Battleground Europe

LOOS – 1915
Hohenzollern Redoubt

Other guides in the Battleground Europe Series:

Walking the Salient *by* Paul Reed
Ypres - Sanctuary Wood and Hooge *by* Nigel Cave
Ypres - Hill 60 *by* Nigel Cave
Ypres - Messines Ridge *by* Peter Oldham
Ypres - Polygon Wood *by* Nigel Cave
Ypres - Passchendaele *by* Nigel Cave
Ypres - Airfields and Airmen *by* Michael O'Connor
Ypres - St Julien *by* Graham Keech

Walking the Somme *by* Paul Reed
Somme - Gommecourt *by* Nigel Cave
Somme - Serre *by* Jack Horsfall & Nigel Cave
Somme - Beaumont Hamel *by* Nigel Cave
Somme - Thiepval *by* Michael Stedman
Somme - La Boisselle *by* Michael Stedman
Somme - Fricourt *by* Michael Stedman
Somme - Carnoy-Montauban *by* Graham Maddocks
Somme - Pozières *by* Graham Keech
Somme - Courcelette *by* Paul Reed
Somme - Boom Ravine *by* Trevor Pidgeon
Somme - Mametz Wood *by* Michael Renshaw
Somme - Delville Wood *by* Nigel Cave
Somme - Advance to Victory (North) 1918 *by* Michael Stedman
Somme - Flers *by* Trevor Pidgeon
Somme - Bazentin Ridge *by* Edward Hancock and Nigel Cave
Somme - Combles *by* Paul Reed

Arras - Vimy Ridge *by* Nigel Cave
Arras - Gavrelle *by* Trevor Tasker and Kyle Tallett
Arras - Bullecourt *by* Graham Keech
Arras - Monchy le Preux *by* Colin Fox

Hindenburg Line *by* Peter Oldham
Hindenburg Line Epehy *by* Bill Mitchinson
Hindenburg Line Riqueval *by* Bill Mitchinson
Hindenburg Line Villers-Plouich *by* Bill Mitchinson
Hindenburg Line - Cambrai, Right Hook *by* Jack Horsfall & Nigel Cave
Hindenburg Line - Saint Quentin *by* Helen McPhail and Philip Guest
Hindenburg Line - Bourlon Wood *by* Jack Horsfall & Nigel Cave

La Bassée - Neuve Chapelle *by* Geoffrey Bridger
Loos - Hohenzollen Redoubt *by* Andrew Rawson
Loos - Hill 70 *by* Andrew Rawson
Mons *by* Jack Horsfall and Nigel Cave
Accrington Pals Trail *by* William Turner

Poets at War: Wilfred Owen *by* Helen McPhail and Philip Guest
Poets at War: Edmund Blunden *by* Helen McPhail and Philip Guest
Poets at War: Graves & Sassoon *by* Helen McPhail and Philip Guest

Gallipoli *by* Nigel Steel

Touring the Italian Front *by* Francis Mackay
Italy - Asiago *by* Francis Mackay

Verdun, Fort Donamont *by* Christina Holstein

Boer War - The Relief of Ladysmith *by* Lewis Childs
Boer War - The Siege of Ladysmith *by* Lewis Childs
Boer War - Kimberley *by* Lewis Childs
Isandlwana *by* Ian Knight and Ian Castle
Rorkes Drift *by* Ian Knight and Ian Castle

***Wars of the Roses* - Wakefield/ Towton** *by* Philip A. Haigh
***English Civil War* - Naseby** *by* Martin Marix Evans, Peter Burton and Michael Westaway
Napoleonic - **Hougoumont** *by* Julian Paget and Derek Saunders
Napoleonic - **Waterloo** *by* Andrew Uffindell and Michael Corum

WW2 **Pegasus Bridge/Merville Battery** *by* Carl Shilleto
WW2 **Utah Beach** *by* Carl Shilleto
WW2 **Gold Beach** *by* Christopher Dunphie & Garry Johnson
WW2 **Normandy - Gold Beach Jig** *by* Tim Saunders
WW2 **Omaha Beach** *by* Tim Kilvert-Jones
WW2 **Sword Beach** *by* Tim Kilvert-Jones
WW2 **Battle of the Bulge - St Vith** *by* Michael Tolhurst
WW2 **Battle of the Bulge - Bastogne** *by* Michael Tolhurst
WW2 **Dunkirk** *by* Patrick Wilson
WW2 **Calais** *by* Jon Cooksey
WW2 **Boulogne** *by* Jon Cooksey
WW2 *Das Reich* **– Drive to Normandy** *by* Philip Vickers
WW2 **Hill 112** *by* Tim Saunders
WW2 **Market Garden - Nijmegen** *by* Tim Saunders
WW2 **Market Garden - Hell's Highway** *by* Tim Saunders
WW2 **Market Garden - Arnhem, Oosterbeek** *by* Frank Steer
WW2 **Market Garden - The Island** *by* Tim Saunders
WW2 **Channel Islands** *by* George Forty

Battleground Europe Series guides under contract for future release:

Stamford Bridge & Hastings *by* Peter Marren
Somme - High Wood *by* Terry Carter
Somme - German Advance 1918 *by* Michael Stedman
Somme - Beaucourt *by* Michael Renshaw
Walking Arras *by* Paul Reed
Gallipoli - Gully Ravine *by* Stephen Chambers
Fromelles *by* Peter Pedersen
Hamel *by* Peter Pedersen
WW2 **Normandy - Epsom** *by* Tim Saunders
WW2 **Normandy - Mont Pinçon** *by* Eric Hunt
WW2 **Normandy - Operation Bluecoat** *by* Ian Daglish
WW2 **Market Garden - Arnhem, The Bridge** *by* Frank Steer
WW2 **Normandy - Falaise** *by* Tim Kilvert-Jones
WW2 **Walcheren** *by* Andrew Rawson

Battleground Europe

LOOS - 1915
Hohenzollern Redoubt

Andrew Rawson

Series Editor
Nigel Cave

LEO COOPER

First published in 2003 by
LEO COOPER
an imprint of
Pen & Sword Books Limited
47 Church Street, Barnsley, South Yorkshire S70 2AS

ISBN 0 85052 903 4

A CIP catalogue record of this book is available
from the British Library

Printed by CPI UK.

For up-to-date information on other titles produced under the Leo Cooper imprint, please telephone or write to:

Pen & Sword Books Ltd, FREEPOST, 47 Church Street
Barnsley, South Yorkshire S70 2AS
Telephone 01226 734222

CONTENTS

Introduction by Series Editor

With this second book on the ill-fated battle of Loos, fought in September and October 1915, a great gap in the coverage of the British Western Front battlefields in the *Battleground Europe* series has been filled. Loos is a rather depressing battle; and it has to be said, it was fought over rather depressing - or at least unrepossessing - countryside.

Loos has been sadly neglected by military historians, and this book helps to fill the gap; though it should be noted that the Official History account is a generally sound one. People, understandly, are put off by the Official History's rather stolid appearance - and of course for many years it was practically unobtainable. Philip Warner's book on Loos (now back in print) was about all that was popularly available in recent years, if one chose to ignore the extraordinary ill-informed *The Donkeys* by the late Alan Clark.

As a battle Loos shows how often British generals in the early years of the war were forced by political imperatives to conduct operations to a considerable extent at the behest of French planning (in the case as a subsidiary action to the Battle of Artois). No British commander at any level wanted to fight a battle there. But that apart, whatever chances of success there might have been were severely impeded by the horrendous shortage of artillery in anything like sufficent quantities and with anything remotely like enough shells (and shells that actually worked, of course). On top of this the errors in the conduct of the operations. Above all, there was the quality of the foe - well disciplined, well trained, well equipped and committed. What the battlefield of Loos does offer, however, is an oasis, for the most part, of open fields in an industrialised setting and a landscape that has not changed dramatically from the events of those autumn days of 1915. Andrew Rawson has provided an excellent and readable account of the battle and then put it all on to today's ground. I have always enjoyed being able to place myself on the site where events took place, and in this Andrew has succeeded admirably. Herioc, if hopeless, attacks by battalions can be traced; VC actions can be viewed, and the tragic stories of the well known (such as Charles Sorley) can be placed in context.

Loos was a battle that came close to success, and failed for the reasons listed above. However, a visit here helps to put the extraordinary achievement of the British nation into context in the raising of its huge citizen army, the most significant fighting force (reinforced by the invaluable contribution of the Dominion members of its Empire) on the continent by the end of 1918. Perhaps you might already have looked at Neuve Chapelle, a few miles to the north - the first major British offensive battle of the war (see Geoff Bridger's *Neuve Chapelle* in this series). It was fought over a tiny front by the standards of the German and French battles of the time. Here at Loos, standing at St Mary's ADS Cemetery, it is easy to view the whole of the British front, itself a large increase on that of Neuve Chapelle. Only nine months or so after Loos it was quite impossible to view the British front of 1st July on the Somme from any vantage point; whilst it would have been unthinkable in September 1915 that the British could engage in a prolonged operation of more than a few weeks - and the Somme lasted four and a half months.

Loos is a haunting battlefield; this book should help to rescue it from obscurity; and - rather more importantly - also the men and the battalions that fought here.

Nigel Cave, *Ely Place, London*

ACKNOWLEDGEMENTS

In common with many visitors to the Western Front, my first encounter with Loos was a brief stop at the Loos Memorial to the Missing. Guided there by Rose Coombes timeless guide, *'Before Endeavours Fade'*, I gave it no more than a fleeting glance before heading south to the Somme. Further detailed visits to Flanders and the Somme left me looking for new areas to explore and a cycling tour of the Loos area followed. My visit convinced me that the battle was worth further investigation; however, apart from a few brief references, there was a dearth of material. The chance acquisition of the Official History of the battle was the start of a five year quest for information. It was obvious from the official version that the battle was an important, albeit short, campaign in the development of the British Army. Even so, as books dedicated to later campaigns continued to roll off the presses, Loos continued to be overlooked.

It has been a personal voyage of discovery to uncover what happened amongst the pit villages east of Bethune over eighty years ago. Even so, many people have assisted me along the way and without their assistance my knowledge of the battle would have been far from complete. Above all the battalion diarists who wrote their version of the battle, often under very difficult conditions, deserve remembering. In many cases they were recording the loss of hundreds of personal friends and without them this book would not contain such a richness of detail.

Over the years, Doctor John Bourne, of the University of Birmingham, has provided encouragement and help during the learning curve of my research. Without his assistance many doors would have remained closed or undiscovered. Martin Middlebrook provided advice at the beginning and his approach to visiting the Western Front has motivated me along the way. During the writing stage, Nigel Cave has coaxed me along, providing practical advice at each stage. Without his help I would have stumbled many times. The staff at the Imperial War Museum guided me through the acres of books and photographs stored at the Lambeth site, tirelessly processing my requests. The same applies to the staff at the Public Record Office at Kew. Without their assistance, a great deal of the information would never have been unearthed. Over the past six months Michelle Taylor has transformed a series of hand written notes into a presentable script. Meanwhile, my partner Amanda has endured endless stories of the battle, listening as I recount details of events that she, as yet, has little interest in. Without these people this book would still only be an idea.

Finally, I dedicate this book to my son Alex, in the hope that his generation never faces the hardships endured by the children born a century before him.

ADVICE TO TOURERS

Visitors to the area around Auchy-lès-Mines and the Hohenzollern Redoubt need to set aside a full day to study the area in detail. The southern half of the battlefield, covering IV Corps operations around Loos, is dealt with in a companion volume. Visitors to the area can choose from a number of options. One of the main routes from the channel ports, the A26, passes within a few miles of the area. It is possible to stop by for a few hours on your way to or from the Somme. Take the Bully-lès-Mines exit off the A26, following the A21 for Lens. After three miles turn onto the N42, signposted for Mazingarbe and Bethune. The road drops quickly into a valley; huge twin slagheaps stand to the left of the road, Loos is to the right. Climbing out of the valley, the Loos Memorial to the Missing stands at the top of the ridge, on the right. Although the memorial stands in the centre of IV corps front, many of the men who died in I Corps battle are remembered here.

Alternatively, if wish to spend longer in the area and stay the night, you can arrange accommodation locally. Lens is a thriving industrial centre, and has numerous hotels catering for most pockets. There are far too many to list here, but there are a number close to the railway station to start from. All the main roads lead eventually to the railway, follow signs for *centre ville* or *la gare*.

Many will prefer to stay in Bethune, home to thousands of British soldiers between 1915 and 1918. Originally, the town was protected by ramparts which were updated by Vauban in the 18th Century. Before the industrial revolution the town relied on busy markets that sold produce collected from the surrounding fertile land. The town also supported a thriving cloth trade. The exploitation of the rich coal seams, south and east of the town, began in the second half of the 19th century. Bethune was again an important centre, serving the host of collieries that sprung up in the area.

War arrived in the town in October 1914. French troops began detraining at the stations in the area as the front expanded north, in the so-called Race to the Sea. Contact with the Germans was made a few miles to the east around La Bassée and Lens. However, the generals' attentions were quickly drawn elsewhere and the trenches east of Bethune were known as a quiet sector. The following spring the expanding British Army moved into the area, taking over the front as far south as Grenay. For the next three and a half years the town was a major centre on First Army's front. The town suffered relatively light

Bethune Belfry, landmark for First Army's men.

Bethune Belfry at the end of the war.

damage at first and many civilians preferred to stay on in their homes, selling goods to the soldiers. In the meantime the collieries behind the lines continued to mine coal, essential for the war effort. On 9 April 1918, the Germans launched a devastating attack north of the La Bassée, and for a time it appeared as though they would overrun Bethune. Eventually, the line stabilised almost at the town gates. During the battle the town was virtually destroyed, ninety percent of the buildings damaged beyond repair. Despite the devastation plans for rebuilding the town in its original style were soon put into practice. Today it is hard to imagine that the town once lay in ruins.

The Belfry in the main square would have been a familiar sight for many soldiers, as they milled around the square in search of mischief in one of the many bars. The original tower was erected in 1346, to act as a watch-tower. A sturdier tower soon replaced the structure and with the addition of an extra floor in 1437, the Belfry became a focal point for the townspeople. For many years a watchman lived in the rooms near the top of the tower to guard against invaders. It was badly damaged during the spring of 1918, and the upper stories were completely destroyed. As the town's main landmark, the Belfry was rebuilt after the war, although the buildings that surrounded the base have not been replicated.

The cobbled square surrounding

the Belfry has retained many of its original buildings and it is not difficult to imagine what it looked like in 1915. During the days before the Battle of Loos the square would have been busy with men looking to enjoy themselves before the 'Big Push'. It is a pleasant place to stay awhile, enjoying a meal or drink at one of the many bars and restaurants. Looking across the square on a warm evening as you discuss your travels, remember what the men of 1915 faced as they enjoyed what was, for many, their last drink.

Experienced travellers will be well-versed in what is required before setting out across the channel. However, the area will be new to many of you and the La Bassée area is quite different to the Somme and Ypres in some ways. Familiarise yourself with the battle before setting out to explore, taking time to study the enclosed maps and any relevant road maps before setting out. It can be an extremely frustrating experience if you rush onto the battlefield unprepared. The area covered is quite small, and it is possible to drive from one end to the other in a matter of minutes.

The early stages of the battle fought across open country, where by the autumn of 1915 neither side had either the time or resources to construct elaborate trench systems. The short duration of the battle means that there are few permanent scars on the landscape. In places craters have been left by the farmers, and are now covered with bushes and undergrowth. It is recommended that you avoid entering such areas, something as simple as a twisted ankle could leave you in a very difficult situation. Hard chalk just beneath the surface enabled deep shelters to be dug, so there are few bunkers in the area. The handful that can be seen are mentioned in the text. Although the battlefield is in the centre of an industrial area, I Corps front has remained relatively unscathed. A few areas have been changed beyond all recognition, in particular the Brickstacks, Fosse 8 and Hulluch Quarries. However, on the whole, the area has changed little.

There are a large number of maps in the book to help you find your way around. However, you may wish to purchase the appropriate IGN Series Blue map (1:25,000). 2405 est - (Lens) which covers the whole battlefield. You may also wish to obtain 2405 ouest (Bethune) which covers the British rear area and Bethune town. These maps are of a similar scale to the 1:20,000 British trench maps and can be extremely helpful for making detailed studies of the area. The CWGC supplies 1:250000 Michelin maps with the British war cemeteries overprinted. They also contain a useful index and cost about £3. There are a number of trench map extracts in the book, however, you may wish to obtain the relevant sheet for the battle. The Western Front Association provides a trench map service for members, the appropriate references are 36cNW1 La Bassée (area north of Hohenzollern Redoubt) and 36cNW3 (area of Hohenzollern Redoubt) Loos.

The shops along the main street of Auchy-lès-Mines will be able to provide most of what you need. However, be warned that the village closes around midday for a long lunch and on certain days closes completely for the afternoon. If you are looking forward to a picnic, make sure that you purchase your food early. Alternatively, La Bassée and Bethune and their supermarkets are only a short distance away by car.

The countryside is gentle and undulating and walking is nearly always easy going. There are a number of short walks detailed in the book so you never need travel far from your car. Stout walking boots and a set of waterproofs (in case the weather turns to rain) should be adequate for your visit. A basic first aid would be advisable to deal with small emergencies (it is a legal requirement to carry one in your vehicle). Take along a supply of bottled water to quench your thirst, particularly on hot days. A few chocolate bars are always welcome to help you on your way. Other useful items include binoculars, a compass and a camera. A notebook to record your photographs is particularly useful; fields can look very much the same when you collect your films from the developers a couple of weeks later.

The area is criss-crossed by numerous tarmac and dirt tracks. Although it may seem a good idea to drive along them, many are dead-ends. Others are deeply rutted and would test the suspension of even the toughest car. The sensible option is to park your vehicle in a safe place and proceed on foot. The tracks are primarily for use by the farmers and should be kept clear at all times. The majority of farmers would not object to them being used if the harvest has been collected, however, if in doubt, ask. If you do wish to stop to study a particular view, do not stray far from your car and be prepared to move at short notice. Above all do not leave your vehicle where it could stop a tractor from passing. When searching for a place to pull over and park, remember that deep ditches can lurk in the long grass alongside the roads.

Never stray into a field which contains standing crops. If, however, you find yourself lost, try at all times to keep to the rough strips of land that seem to act as boundary lines in this area. Unlike the Somme, the locals are not used to British visitors. If you happen to be caught out, be prepared for a long explanation in French. There are a few areas of

Wartime debris still litters the battlefield.

woodland, some of which conceal deep craters from the Great War. The best advice is to stay out. Some of the copses are used by farmers as dumping grounds for the scrap found in the fields. Mining companies, or one of the other local industries, fenced off several private areas. Again, keep out. It is possible to view virtually all the battlefield from many angles, so there is no need to enter private land. Remember that the sign 'Privé' denotes private land.

Thousands of artillery shells were fired during and after the battle, and the area is still scattered with those that failed to explode. Steer clear of any you may come across, shells were designed to kill and injure and some are still capable of doing so. It is illegal to use a metal detector on someone else's property and you could find yourself in serious trouble if you are found digging for relics.

Relevant sources

Both the National Army Museum and the Imperial War Museum are worth a visit before embarking for France. They have a variety of interesting exhibits and displays relevant to World War One. The IWM in particular has a well-stocked bookshop. There is a comprehensive collection of divisional and regimental histories in the IWM library, many with references to the battle. All that is needed is an appointment, arranged either by telephone or letter; although some indication of what you wish to view helps the staff find items before your arrival. A Reader's Ticket is needed for the NAM library; take suitable identification to acquire one.

Every unit was obliged to complete a daily diary, and they are kept in the Public Record's Office. It is well worth a visit to Kew if you are interested in the Great War, just for the experience of viewing original documents. Although the building is rather daunting, the staff will soon help you come to grips with the modern catalogue system. Individual army records are also stored at Kew, although many were destroyed during the blitz. The PRO's publication, *Army Service Records of the First World War,* is a useful introduction to the information available.

Although there is no need for an appointment, take suitable identification to obtain a reader's card. Those of you with internet experience may find the PRO's website of interest. Although you cannot view documents online, it is possible to browse the catalogue from home. (search for ***pro***). War diaries are catalogued under WO95 (War Office - section 95).

If you wish to search for details relating to a particular casualty, the Commonwealth War Graves Commission is usually able to assist. If you are able to supply details of name, rank, regiment and approximate date of death, the CWGC can check their records. They are normally able to supply the whereabouts of the individual's grave, or the memorial that they are remembered on. There may be a charge for written requests, according to the circumstances of the enquiry. The CWGC also has a website (search for ***cwgc***) which grants access to the Debt of Honour Register. It is well worth investigating; enlist a computer literate friend if you are unable to use the internet. It is also possible to search the CWGC's records at their France area office. It is situated at Beaurains, on the southern outskirts of Arras. The work carried out by the CWGC never ceases to amaze, and the care taken by their employees in maintaining the cemeteries and memorials enhances any trip to the Western Front. Take time to express your thanks in the visitor's books that are kept in the larger cemeteries. They are particularly appreciated where visitors are few and far between.

A few basic, yet essential, items are needed before you cross the channel. You need registration and insurance documents for your vehicle. Although the Green Card system seems to have lapsed as Europe becomes one, it is wise to check with your insurance company first. It is compulsory to carry a warning triangle, a first aid kit and spare light bulbs. Also make sure you stick the self-adhesive deflectors to your headlights as you wait at the ferry terminal. Always have your passport and driving license to hand in case the police perform a stop check on your vehicle. Although the local wines and beers are very tasty and reasonably priced, drivers are advised to abstain until the evening. The drink driving laws are stricter than in the UK, and it will take your full concentration to navigate around the area.

Visitors to France are recommended to obtain full medical and health insurance. Although the E111 form (available from main post offices) does provide reciprocal cover, it does not cover every eventuality. In some instances you may find yourselves with a hefty medical bill.

Hotels

Accommodation can usually be found without difficulty in Bethune. However, there is a carnival on the weekend nearest 3 September, Liberation Day in 1944, and many hotels are booked up well in advance. The following is a sample and some may close, whilst new ones open over the course of time. The Tourist information office (Tel: +33 321 57 25 47), situated in the Grand Place on the ground floor of the Belfry, will be able to provide an up to date list:

Hotel du Vieux Beffroi, Grand Place, Bethune
Tel: +33 321 68 15 00
Hotel de la Coupole, Grand Place, Bethune
Tel: +33 321 57 35 01
Hotel Bernard, Place de la Gare, Bethune
Tel: +33 321 57 20 02
Tour Hotel du Golf, RN43, (Rond-point St-Pry), Bethune
Tel: +33 321 56 90 00

There are also a number of hotels in the outlying suburbs; Fouquereuil and Fouquieres to the south and Beuvry to the east.

Many hotels have restaurants, but if not, the town is overflowing with cafés and restaurants. Take a wander and find one that appeals to your palate and your pocket.

Useful addresses

The Imperial War Museum,
Lambeth, London SE1 6H2.
Tel: 020 7416 5000

The National Army Museum,
Royal Hospital Road, Chelsea, London SW3 4HT.
Tel: 020 7730 0717

The Commonwealth War Graves Commission,
2 Marlow Road, Maidenhead, Berks
Tel: 01628 634221

The Western Front Association,
PO Box 1914, Reading, Berks.
This is the address for membership enquiries. Include a large (A4) stamped addressed envelope.

How to use this book

A little forward planning is advised if the Bethune area is new to you. Before leaving for France, take time to read through the book (and any from the further reading section you can acquire) to get a feel for the battle. In many respects it differed considerably from the prolonged battles in Flanders and on the Somme. The Battle of Loos in September 1915 was a short, but bloody, battle in which the British Army learnt many crucial lessons. Although there is a need for a full account of the battle, this book is not intended to be a comprehensive history. It will, however, give the reader a feel for the events that took place on I Corps front.

It is possible to tour the area covered in this book by car in an hour or so. However, the best means of getting around is on foot. Walking allows the visitor the time to take in the surroundings, stopping to take in the view or refer to the book at leisure. It is impossible to view the battlefield while concentrating on the road. Although the road network makes it very difficult to walk across the entire area in one go, there are plenty of paths to choose from. The recommended way to visit I Corps area is to drive from point to point, stopping along the way to walk onto the battlefield. Some choose to tour on bicycles, a practical compromise. However, there are difficulties. The major roads in the area can be extremely busy and cycle paths are few and far between.

Chapter One

PLANNING THE OFFENSIVE

First Army's offensive east of Bethune was part of a wider scheme of operations designed to push the Germans from French soil. Planning for the offensive began even before the Battle of Artois had ended. General Joffre's strategy involved attacking two points in the German line. The first would strike across the open Champagne region, driving north towards the Ardennes. The second thrust was to drive east, across the Artois region, in the hope of de-stabilising the German line south of Lens. If successful the two advances would converge, threatening the flanks of the salient between the River Somme and the River Aisne. It was an optimistic plan, and Joffre wanted British support.

Field Marshal Sir John French.

Field Marshal Sir John French received Joffre's proposals at the beginning of June. In order to build up a reserve, the British were expected to take over responsibility for the line north of the River Somme. He also requested that the British co-operated with their own offensive, directed against the German line north of Lens. French accepted the proposal, for with the arrival of the territorial and New Army divisions his army was strong enough to strike. General Haig, First Army's commander, was to prepare a scheme in line with Joffre's scheme. He was not

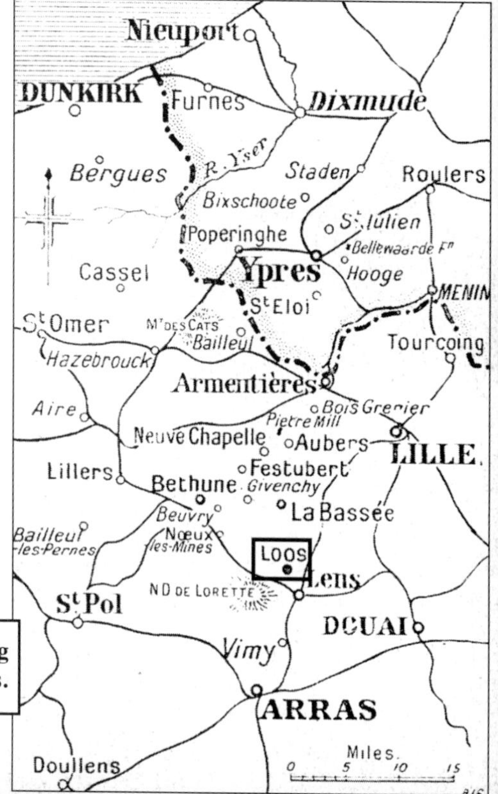

Map 1. The Western Front, showing Loos in relation to Ypres and Arras.

convinced. The ground south of the La Bassée canal was flat and open; villages, which could be easily fortified, dotted the plain. Haig advised against the operation and suggested that First Army would have a greater chance of success north of the canal.

At the end of June 1915 the French and British general staffs held a conference at Boulogne to discuss the forthcoming year. The conclusions were discouraging. The spring offensives had been launched on narrow frontages that had been easily contained by a small reserve. What was needed was an attack along a broad front, up to fifteen miles wide, to breach the German line effectively. However, the British Army would not be strong enough until the spring of 1916, by which time many more New Army divisions would be ready. Another factor was heavy artillery. Both staffs recognised that large quantities of guns and ammunition would be required to support such an attack. Figures supplied by representatives from the respective munitions industries proved that demand far exceeded supply.

Although the Boulogne conference advised waiting until the spring of 1916 before launching an offensive, General Joffre was determined to strike at the first opportunity. At the St Omer conference on 11 July he announced his intention to attack as soon as the British had taken over the Somme front. Joffre wanted assurances that the British Army would be able to support him, however, French refused to be committed. He would only co-operate if the German line south of Lens had been broken first.

Three weeks later at the Frevént conference Joffre asked for British assistance a second time. Again he failed to obtain full support for his plan and despite a stream of correspondence French refused to be bullied into committing his men. In frustration, General Joffre adopted a diplomatic approach aimed at side-stepping the British commander. On 16 August Lord Kitchener visited Joffre's headquarters and although there are no records of the meeting a 'deal' was made. Three days later Kitchener instructed Field Marshal French to *'take the offensive and act vigorously'*.

Although French was displeased by the way he had been over-ruled, Kitchener was no doubt influenced by the global situation. During the summer of 1915 the allies suffered a number of grievous setbacks. The Dardenelles operation, designed to knock Turkey out of the war, had been a failure. Meanwhile, Italy was reeling from a disastrous attack on Austro-Hungarian forces. In the east the Central Powers Brest-Litovsk offensive had driven the Russians back hundreds of miles. Decisive action was needed on the Western Front to divert the Germans attention and give a morale boost to the Allied cause. Although GHQ did not want the attack and it was not on their chosen ground, the British Army had to show support for its allies. In Kitchener's own words;

> .... *we must act with all energy and do our utmost to help France in their offensive, even though by doing so we may suffer heavy losses.*

Without sufficient heavy artillery, First Army had to look elsewhere for assistance. The Germans had demonstrated in April how gas could be used to create panic, ripping a huge hole in the line north of Ypres. During the summer British scientists had developed a similar weapon. For the first time British troops would use gas as an offensive weapon.

General Sir Douglas Haig.

Throughout August the roads and railways around Bethune were crammed with troops moving into the area. It was going to be the British Army's largest offensive battle so far and the first in which Kitchener's New Army divisions would be used.

There was, however, a problem. If the wind speed proved insufficient for the deployment of gas the assault troops would be extremely vulnerable. Recognising his dependence on the weather, General Haig prepared two plans. If gas could be used, First Army would strike with the six divisions of I Corps and IV Corps. XI Corps, with three infantry divisions, would be available to exploit the breakthrough. Four cavalry divisions would deliver the final blow. Meanwhile, the Indian and III Corps would carry out subsidiary attacks north of the La Bassée canal. General Plumer's Second Army would also attack in Flanders, in the hope of pinning down German reserves. If the weather failed to allow the deployment of gas, First Army would only attack with two divisions on the first day. The 9th (Scottish) Division would capture Hohenzollern Redoubt and Fosse 8 on I Corps front. Meanwhile, on IV Corps front, the 15th (Scottish) Division would seize two strongpoints in the German line, Loos Road and Lens Road Redoubts. Haig would then monitor the weather for the next forty-eight hours, launching the full weight of his force as soon as the wind turned in his favour.

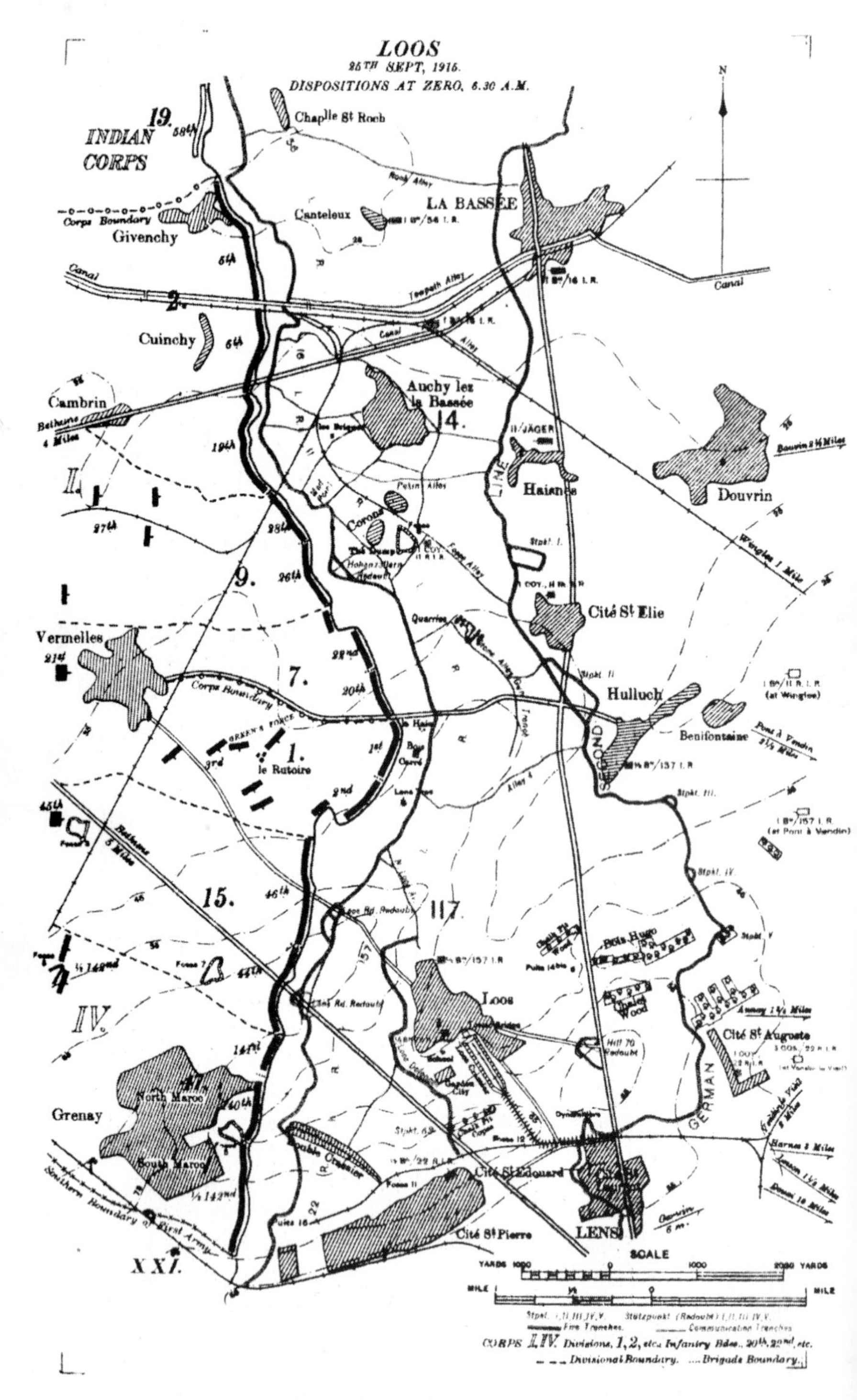

First Army's deployment at zero hour.

Chapter Two

THE BATTLEFIELD IN 1915

Lieutenant-General Sir Hubert Gough.

Lieutenant-General Hubert Gough's I Corps faced an area that had been scarred by the industrial revolution. Since the discovery of coal in the nineteenth century, the area west of La Bassée had become home to a number of collieries, known as Fosses. Mining villages, composed of a mixture of pithead buildings and poorly built houses, soon appeared. As work continued underground huge slagheaps sprung up, dominating the skyline. Meanwhile, farmers continued to till the soil on the unaffected areas.

The front held by I Corps ran approximately north to south, in a flattened 'S' shape. It skirted Auchy-lès-Mines and Fosse 8 before swinging south to the Vermelles - Hulluch road. Using three divisions, I

Panoramic view of I Corps front.

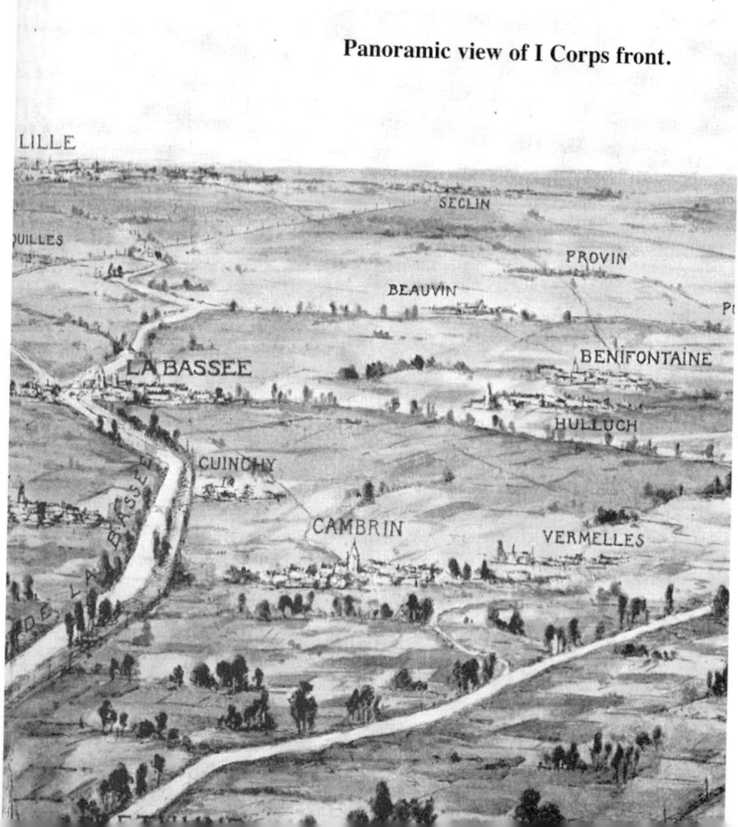

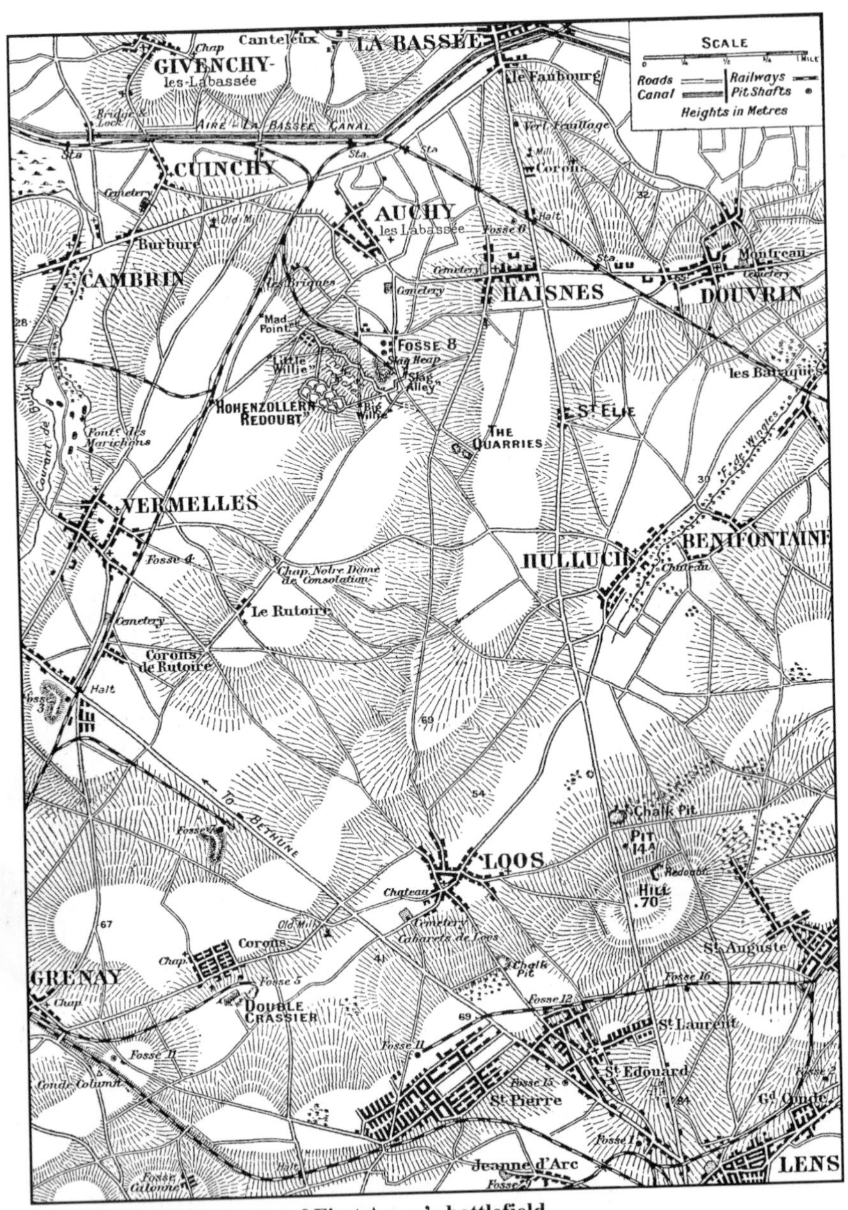

Topographical map of First Army's battlefield.

Corps attack would develop eastwards, with the left hand division holding a refused flank facing La Bassée. Lieutenant-General Henry Rawlinson's IV Corps would advance on Gough's right with three divisions. 1st Division would capture Hulluch on I Corps' southern flank, while 15th (Scottish) Division advanced through Loos.

Meanwhile, 47th (London) Division would form a refused flank facing the northern suburbs of Lens.

First Army also had a strong reserve to call upon, three divisions of XI Corps and a single cavalry division. 21st Division was camped near Beuvry, five miles behind I Corps front, while 24th Division was stationed around Nouex-les-Mines, six miles behind IV Corps. The two divisions were expected to advance into open country. The Guards Division was billeted to the west of Bethune as the final reserve. The 3rd Cavalry Division would be ready to exploit any breakthrough. The Cavalry Corps was waiting twenty miles behind First Army's front, ready to deliver the final blow.

What follows is a description of the ground covered by each of I Corps' divisions, combined with an outline of First Army's plan. Each part starts in the division's rear area, working east across No Man's Land as far as the high water mark of the British advance, in some cases close to or at the German second line of defence. Major-General Horne's 2nd Division held I Corps left flank. The Divisional front was cut in half by the La Bassée Canal, a deep water canal connecting the coalfield with the coast. The troops on the north side of the canal were expected to form a protective flank between Givenchy and La Bassée, while the rest of the Division pushed east through Auchy-lès-Mines. Givenchy stands just behind the British front line on a low hill overlooking the surrounding area. The front line ran through flat

I Corps deployment and objectives, also shows detail of German defences.

featureless fields, where the water table was never far from the surface. Two small hamlets, Chapelle St Roch and Canteleux, marked the limits of the Divisional objectives north of the canal.

The canal runs through a shallow cutting as it crosses the front line, and material excavated during the construction work was deposited on the north bank. In 1915 the German front line incorporated one of the spoil heaps, turning it into a formidable strongpoint known as The Tortoise.

South of the canal there are two villages just behind the British front, Cuinchy and Cambrin A railway line runs along the southern bank of the canal and as it crossed the front line the tracks are elevated on a low embankment. A German strongpoint dug under the railway was known as Embankment Redoubt. Just south of the railway was one of the most notorious sectors on the Western Front, the Brickstacks. The front line ran through the stockyard of a brickworks and by the autumn of 1915 the piles of bricks had been converted into strongpoints. Edmund Blunden stayed in the area in 1916 and his recollections of the sector appear in Chapter IV of his autobiography, *Undertones of War*:

> *Cuinchy was a slaughter-yard. My ignorance carried me through it with less ado than I can now understand. The front line, which C Company in a few nights occupied, was in many*

Men of the South Staffordshires in the Brickstacks sector. IWM - Q47576

ways singular. It ran through an extensive brickfield, with many foursquare brickstacks, fused into solidity; of these historic strange monuments about a dozen lay in our lines, and about the same in the German lines. The brickstacks, such as them that were occupied, were approached by insecure, narrow windings, through a wicked clay; our domestic arrangements naturally grouped themselves on the home side of them, and no less naturally the Germans at their discretion belaboured them and their precincts with high-explosive. The deep dug-outs behind them were not quite deep enough, but to anyone arriving there the sight of a smoky black stairway down, with equipment suspended like trophies at the entrance, was better than what Moses saw from Pisgah.

A railway junction, connecting the local collieries with the main line, occupied the ground to the east of the Brickstacks.

Soon after the front stabilised in October 1914, both sides started to dig underground south of the canal. The Cuinchy sector was particularly hated because of the mining activity. By September 1915 No Man's Land was filled with a necklace of deep mine craters and on the right of 2nd Division's front the advance would be severely affected by mining activity. In many places the craters almost completely filled the area between the trenches and the assault troops would have to funnel through the gaps between them.

The German trenches opposite Major-General Henry Horne's front were particularly strong, designed to protect Auchy-lès-Mines from attack. The main support line ran along the Vermelles railway line, while a second series of trenches ran around the outskirts of the

2nd Division's front south of the La Bassée canal, Auchy-lès-Mines can be seen in the distance to the right of the photograph. IWM - Q37763

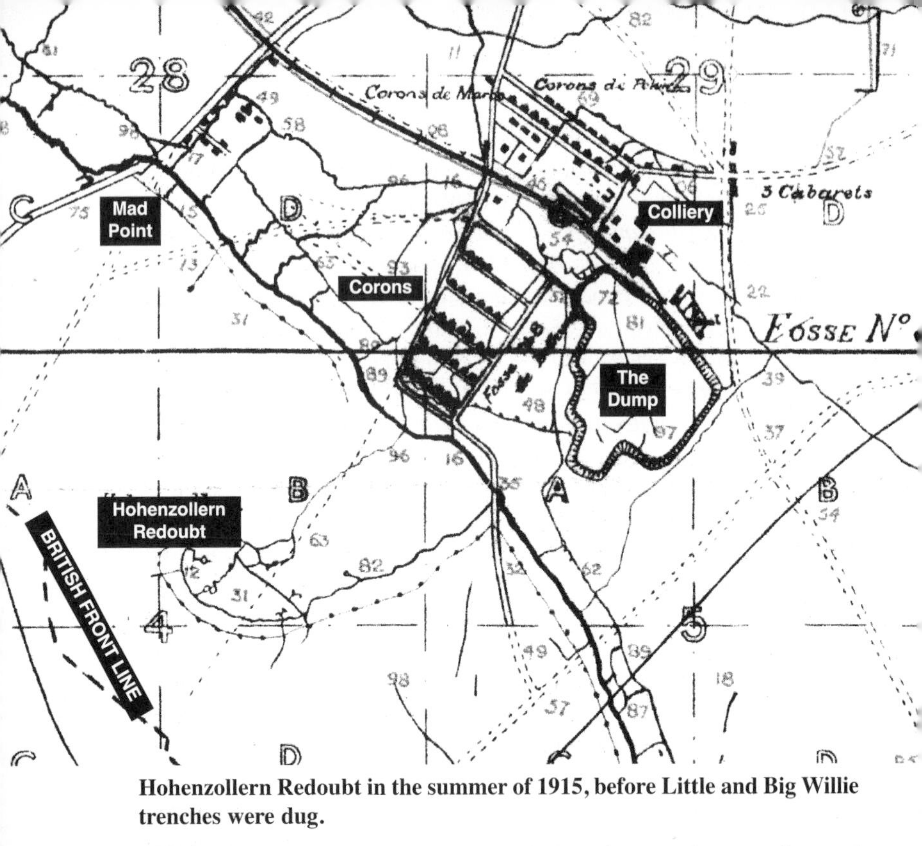

Hohenzollern Redoubt in the summer of 1915, before Little and Big Willie trenches were dug.

village. A number of emplacements, designed to conduct an all round defence, dotted the fields. Having taken the northern half of Auchy, Horne's men would push east. The plan called for a defensive flank facing the town of La Bassée. The centre of the Division would make

The centre of I Corps front. Auchy is on the left, while Fosse 8 colliery and the Dump occupy the centre of the landscape. Cité St Elie is on the right. IWM - Q37764

a stand along the Lens railway line, immediately south of the La Bassée Canal. The right had to assist the 9th (Scottish) Division in clearing Haisnes before establishing a line east of the village.

The front held by Major-General George Thesiger's 9th (Scottish) Division, in the centre of I Corps front, was fraught with difficulties. The left of the division straddled the Vermelles - Auchy road, close to a hamlet known as Madagascar. At this point the two front lines were about two hundred metres apart, facing each other across open fields. A large strongpoint, known as Mad Point protruded from the front line where the trenches crossed the road. Having taken the front line trenches, the assault troops would head north east astride the Auchy road, crossing the Fosse 8 colliery railway line. The Germans had dug two support lines to cover Auchy from the south, where the Division was expected to enter the village. As Thesiger's men made their way through the streets, they were expected to link up with 2nd Division before heading east towards Haisnes.

No Man's Land was originally four hundred metres wide on the right of 9th Division's sector, with a low ridge separating the trenches. The Germans had managed to occupy the rise at an early stage, building Hohenzollern Redoubt on the summit. At first, the redoubt formed a large enclosed keep overlooking the Allied trenches. The fire trench curved around the contours of the land, while communications trenches ran back towards the front line. A few weeks before the battle the Germans dug new fire trenches to incorporate the redoubt into the front line. They were known as Big Willie and Little Willie Trench, the nicknames afforded to the Kaiser and the Crown Prince by British troops.

IWM - Q37765

The original German front line ran along the southern outskirts of Fosse 8 mining commune. The pithead, with its winding tower, coal bunkers, offices and railway sidings, formed the nucleus of the colliery. Half a dozen rows of cottages, known as Corons, stood to the north west and south west. A huge slagheap, known to the troops as 'The Dump', spread across the fields south of the mine. Standing at six metres high, its flat top acted as an important viewing platform for artillery observers. Deep dugouts, burrowed into the slag, protected the soldiers from danger.

Once the colliery had been cleared, the right of the division would head for the gap between Haisnes and Cité St Elie. The ground rises gently beyond Fosse 8 and at the top stood the German Second Line. Thesiger's men would have to cross 1,000 metres of open ground under fire if any Germans occupied the line. The trench skirted the western edge of Haisnes before heading south towards Cité St Elie. *Stutzpunkt* I, an entrenched fort, covered the gap between the two villages. Once Thesiger's men had captured this line, they would be able to head east through Douvrin, making for the Haute Deule Canal.

Major-General Thomson Capper's 7th Division held I Corps' southern sector, with 1st Division (the left hand division of IV Corps) on its right. The ground immediately to its rear consisted of flat, open fields, and it had been impossible to conceal the increase in military traffic prior to the battle. Vermelles stood about a mile west of the front, and many of 7th Division's support troops shared the village with the 1st Division. The village chateau, at the southern end of the village, served as an advanced dressing station during the war; another ADS occupied the cellars of the village brewery. Throughout the battle the

Panorama of 7th Division's front, Cité St Elie is on the horizon to the left of the photograph. IMW - Q37766

British artillerymen in action.

village played host to a number of divisional headquarters, and the streets were filled with troops moving to and from the front. Two of the tallest structures in the village, the church and the water tower, provided observation platforms for artillery spotters.

7th Division's front line faced east and ran along the bottom of an open slope. In the days before the attack, Capper's men had dug a network of assembly trenches in No Man's Land. Although this halved the width of open ground they would have to cross, the German trenches were still over four hundred yards away. There was no cover to protect the assault troops, except for a scattering of unkempt crops that had run wild. Meanwhile, the Germans waited near the top of the slope, watching every move.

Having cleared the front line, the assault troops had to cross the flat summit of the Grenay Ridge. Although there is hardly any change in gradient, the subtle difference in height made all the difference to observation. The ground beyond the crest was uncharted territory for the ground troops and the artillery had relied on aerial observation, a science that was still in its infancy. Just beyond the crest, on the left of the Divisional front, was Hulluch Quarries, a labyrinth of shallow open-cast mine workings. The front line battalion headquarters operated from deep dug-outs concealed in the quarry. A series of gun pits had been dug into the reverse slope straddling the Hulluch road, facing the right of Capper's front. The guns they protected would be able to target the assault troops as they crossed No Man's Land.

Opposite the centre of the Division was Cité St Elie, a mining community centred on Puits 18. Although the village only consisted of a few irregular rows of cottages, it posed a major obstacle. Many of the houses concealed dug-outs in their basements, and the British artillery had been unable to target them. The village was built astride the main Lens - La Bassée highway, which ran north to south across the battlefield. The colliery stood to the east of the road.

The main concern on 7th Division's sector was the German Second Line, which formed a protective barrier around Cité St Elie. It had been positioned to cover the exposed rear slope, guarding against a breakthrough. The section on the left of the Divisional front, west of the village, was known as Cité Trench. Troops in the trench would be able to fire on troops attempting to advance from the Quarries. South of the village, the trench cut across the Lens road heading for Hulluch, and was known as Puits Trench on British maps. The gap between Cité St Elie and Hulluch was covered by *Stutzpunkt* II, a strongpoint positioned to prevent anyone crossing the Lens road.

If Capper's troops managed to take the Second Line, the left of the Division had to capture Cité St Elie colliery before it faced open countryside. Meanwhile, the troops on the right would have to co-operate with 1st Division to clear the eastern end of Hulluch village.

Chapter Three

THE MEN

The three divisions earmarked to lead I Corps assault had varied experiences of warfare. What follows is a brief background charting the divisions' movements since the outbreak of war.

2nd Division

2nd Division mobilised at Aldershot on the opening day of the war, and left for France a few days later with the rest of the British Expeditionary Force. During the retreat from Mons, the Division remained relatively unscathed, despite a number of rear-guard actions, chiefly at Landrecies and in the Villers-Cotterêts Forest. However, following the German retreat to the Aisne, Major-General C C Monro's command became heavily engaged on the north bank of the river. 2nd Division's real test came in October, when it was called upon to defend the Polygon Wood sector of the Ypres Salient. Repeated attacks reduced the division to a mere skeleton; a number of battalions suffering ninety percent casualties before they were relieved. Reservists recalled to the colours brought the Division back up to strength as autumn turned to winter. Three territorial battalions joined the Division at the end of November.

The start of 1915 saw the arrival of a new commanding officer, Major-General Henry Horne. For several months the Division held the

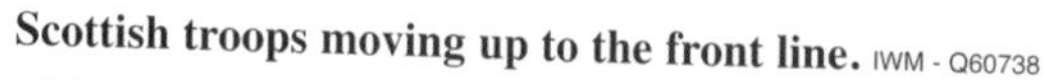

Scottish troops moving up to the front line. IWM - Q60738

La Bassée Canal sector at Givenchy and throughout February it was engaged in a fierce struggle in an area known as the Brickstacks. It was an area many were to fear later in the year. In May Horne's men were called upon to lead an assault on the German line south of Richebourg, in what became know as the Battle of Festubert. On the night of the 15th, 6 Brigade managed to enter the enemy trenches by advancing silently across No Man's Land. Further attacks over the next forty-eight hours failed to dislodge the Germans, and by the time the Division withdrew it had suffered over 5,000 casualties.

Shortly afterwards the Division took over the trenches west of Loos from the French. Lieutenant-General Rawlinson's IV Corps would launch its attack from these trenches on 25 September. However, 2nd Division was needed back in its old sector astride the La Bassée Canal, returning to it at the end of June. It stayed here, apart from brief periods of rest, until the attack three months later.

In August 4 (Guards) Brigade left to join the new Guards Division, forming near St Omer. In its place, 2nd Division welcomed 19 Brigade from 27th Division. The Brigade had been in France since the beginning, acting independently during the retreat from Mons. It joined 6th Division during October and over the next six months held various sectors south of Armentières. Shortly after the Second Battle of Ypres the Brigade joined 27th Division, bolstering the shattered formation while it was brought back up to strength. It joined 2nd Division as it prepared for the forthcoming battle.

9th (Scottish) Division

The 9th (Scottish) Division had the proud distinction of the being the senior division of the First New Army. Throughout August 1914 volunteers signed up from all parts of the Highlands and Lowlands in response to Kitchener's call to arms. By the end of the month there were enough men to furnish more than one division and, before long, the eager recruits were heading south to Salisbury Plain and its vast training area. Settling into their billets around Bordon, the men quickly adapted to army life as they were organised into battalions. Ranks were soon awarded and, although there was a surplus of budding officers amongst the crowd, many preferred to stay with their pals, serving as privates. In one case a company consisted entirely of undergraduates from Glasgow University.

There were, however, far too many recruits for a single Scottish division. On 11th September Army Order No. 382 authorised a second New Army, and the surplus formed the nucleus of the 15th (Scottish)

Scottish recruits.

Division. By chance the two divisions were destined to spearhead First Army's attack, the 9th under I Corps while the 15th served with IV Corps. Loos was going to be a Scottish battle.

The 9th Division was fortunate, having first pick of arms and equipment at a time when demand far exceeded supply. Even so the early stages of training consisted of endless route marches dressed in their civilian clothes, much to the amusement of the local population. At the end of January Major-General H J S Landon, who had seen active service with 1st Division since the outbreak of war, took command. His experience was invaluable in turning the recruits into soldiers and on 5 May the Division paraded on Ludshott Common before their mentor, Field Marshal Earl Kitchener. Two days later embarkation orders arrived and the men said their last good-byes before leaving for the coast. Within a week they were billeted in the villages south west of St Omer, sampling the delights of France.

After three weeks of acclimatisation the men were moved east to Bailleul, from where they could hear the sound of gunfire for the first time. At the beginning of July the Scots took over the Festubert sector north of the La Bassée Canal, experiencing the horrors of the trenches first hand. Two months later the Division moved into reserve to train for the battle ahead, billeting in the villages west of Bethune. On 9 September Major-General George Thesiger, a veteran of the 1898 Nile Expedition and the Boer War, took command. Thesiger had considerable experience and had recently led 2 Brigade during the Battle of Aubers Ridge in May 1915.

7th Division

Although 7th Division was composed of regular battalions, it did not exist before the war. It was formed during August 1914, using battalions recalled from overseas stations in the Mediterranean and

Troops move forward to the trenches. IWM - Q60734

South Africa. At the beginning of October the Division was despatched to Antwerp under the leadership of Major-General Thompson Capper, a veteran of several campaigns in the Sudan and South Africa. The intention was to aid the Belgian Army. However, events overtook the planned operation, and within days of landing the Division was forced to retire. It met the rest of the BEF east of Ypres, helping to stave off the incessant attacks on the Salient. For three weeks Capper's men bore the brunt of countless German attacks and, by the time 7th Division withdrew, eighty-five percent of its fighting strength had been lost.

After a quiet winter holding the line south of Armentières, the Division spearheaded the BEF's attack north of Neuve Chapelle on 10 March. Although the German line was broken with relative ease, blundering led to the attack faltering. 7th Division suffered a high casualty rate in the fighting that followed. On 1 April Capper was injured during experimental tests with hand-grenades. During his absence Major-General Hubert Gough (I Corps commander during the Battle of Loos) led the Division through a number of engagements. On 16 May the division carried out a dawn assault, capturing the German front line north-east of Festubert. Even so, the attack broke down at an early stage and over the following three days casualties mounted as the Division struggled to capitalise on its early success. Over 1,300 men lost their lives; a further 2,700 were wounded. There was little respite;

on 16 June the Division advanced over the same ground in the ill-conceived Action at Givenchy. The attack gained nothing, except to further reduce the shattered Division. In six months it had lost nearly twice its paper strength.

On 19 July Capper returned to his old command, in time to prepare for the anticipated autumn offensive. The Division spent the next few weeks holding sectors north of the La Bassée canal before moving into reserve west of Bethune. During this period hundreds of reservists joined the Division and by September it was back to full strength, ready for action.

THE GERMANS

Very often the Germans are overlooked in studies. Yet time and again, British attacks were brought to a stop by the resilience of the German soldier. The men facing I Corps were out numbered six to one, and faced shell, bullet and gas. Even so they either held out to the last or fell back to occupy their reserve positions. On several occasions small groups held up many times their number, in the hope that reinforcements were on the way, rather than retreating.

I Corps faced elements of two German divisions. 14th Division was mobilised under Second Army, participating in the siege of Liége at the beginning of August 1914. For the next four weeks it marched south, in pursuit of the French Fifth Army. However, by the time it became engaged on the Petit Morin river, Second Army was exhausted and in danger of being outflanked. Moving rapidly north, 14th Division

Germans resting in Hulluch Quarries.

managed to cross the River Aisne and take up positions on the Chemin des Dames. However, within days the division was transferred north to Lille, to take part in the so called Race to the Sea. Plans to outflank the Allies failed to materialise and 14th Division came into contact with French troops west of La Bassée. It remained in the area for the next twelve months, occupying various sectors either side of the La Bassée canal. In March 1915 elements of the division managed to contain the British attack at Neuve Chapelle, and three months later the division thwarted a second attack near Festubert. On 25 September, 14th Division held the line astride the canal, facing General Horne's 2nd Division. One battalion of 56th Regiment occupied the trenches north of the canal, while the support battalion rested in Canteleux. Meanwhile, 16th Regiment held the line south of the canal. The support and reserve battalions were stationed at the Railway Triangle and in La Bassée respectively.

In the spring of 1915 many German divisions were reduced from four to three regiments. 117th Division was formed from the pool of surplus regiments at Liart, in Seventh Army's area of operations. Soon afterwards the division was transferred to the Artois region, in response to French attacks south of Lens. In the weeks that followed 117th Division suffered over 5,500 causalities in fighting near Souchez and Notre Dame Lorette. Following a brief rest in the suburbs of Lille, the division took over responsibility for the sector west of Loos. There was, however, little time to rest. Throughout the summer the men worked around the clock to improve the trenches. They also added a second line of defence to strengthen the front. It connected the fortified villages of Haisnes, Cité St Elie and Hulluch. It was hoped that the support and reserve battalions could hold this line if the British broke through.

On 25 September the 11th Reserve Regiment held the line facing both the 9th (Scottish) Division and 7th Division. Two companies held the front line; the remaining companies occupied Hulluch Quarries and Cité St Elie. The support battalion was split; half stationed at Fosse 8 colliery, while the remainder also occupied Cité St Elie. The third battalion was billeted in Wingles, three miles from the front line. The divisional Jäger Battalion was positioned in Haisnes.

The two divisions would be expected to hold on for at least twenty-four hours. The nearest division to the front was the 2nd Guard Reserve, billeted at Allenes, seven miles east of La Bassée.

GAS OPERATIONS

Chlorine gas was used as on offensive weapon for the first time in April 1915. Germany had shown that chemical warfare was one possible solution to breaking the deadlock on the Western Front. Although the British condemned its use, both the War Office and the Army noted the success. Lord Kitchener immediately appointed Colonel Lois Jackson RE to conduct a feasibility study. The research team at the Imperial College of Science quickly concluded that chlorine could be despatched from pressurised cylinders to form a 'gas cloud'. Using a soda-siphon system, the gas could escape under pressure controlled by a simple stop-cock. A half inch diameter iron pipe (copper was preferred but was in short supply), three metres long, would deliver the liquid chlorine, which would develop into a yellowish white gas as it emerged into the atmosphere.

Side view of a gas mask.

At the beginning of June 1915 the first cylinders were ready for testing. The initial trials were carried out at Runcorn before a select panel from the War Office. Employees from the Castner-Keller factory stood at intervals along the test site, equipped with a smoke-helmet and signalling flag. They would signal as soon as the gas reached them, and then time how long they could stand the poison before they needed the hood; a barbaric, but effective form of measurement. Tests had shown that German gas masks were capable of protecting a man for thirty minutes.

The experiment impressed the War Office and plans were sanctioned for using chlorine gas at the next available opportunity. There was, however, a problem. Calculations showed that the British chemical industry was incapable of producing the quantities required for the length of front proposed. Smoke candles would have to be used to supplement the gas attack, creating the illusion of a continuous cloud of chlorine.

A new gas unit, known as the Special Brigade was formed under Lieutenant-Colonel Foulkes. Throughout the summer, the War Office contacted chemistry students with a view to recruiting them. Students who had already enlisted were drafted across to the Special Brigade under a cloud of secrecy. The men arrived at Helfaut depot, near St

Machine-gun team equipped with gas masks.

Omer, with no idea what was expected of them. Once the project had been explained, each man was given the option of leaving, nearly everyone remained. A large number of the students had no experience of military life and, with little time to spare, Foulkes set about training his men. Crash courses in pistol shooting and navigation came first, followed by lessons on predicting the strength and direction of wind. A forty-eight hour tour of the front line followed (the only time the men entered the trenches prior to the battle).

As training progressed, Foulkes was frantically collecting equipment, pursuing suppliers who often promised more than they could deliver. He was also called upon to attend a number of Army conferences where he was met with a mixture of interest and cynicism.

Meanwhile all along the front preparations were being made. Trains transported the cylinders from the coast to Gorre siding where they readied for action. Lieutenant A B White, officer in charge of the sector astride the La Bassée road, describes how the cylinders were prepared.

> *All arrangements for carrying the cylinders into the trenches were in the hands of the Brigade* [6 Brigade]. *My men were solely responsible for placing them in the trenches. The cylinders were all in wooden boxes in a train. The latter was shunted into a siding at Gorre, where the arrangements were that a fatigue party of one sergeant and ten corporals from each section should unscrew all the boxes, remove the cylinders and loosen the dome covers. The cylinders were then to be replaced in their boxes and only one screw inserted.*

Lorries transported the cylinders to Cambrin Church, where fatigue parties took over. Three or four men carried the cylinders, weighing up to 160lbs each, along the slippery trenches to the front line. Although the whole operation had been veiled in secrecy, the men knew what the code name 'Accessory Number One' stood for. They hated carrying the mystery cylinders, struggling and straining through the narrow trenches. Fortunately, there were no incidents and by the night of the 24th nearly 1,500 cylinders were in place.

Meanwhile, the front line soldiers had been busy preparing for the Special Brigade. Where possible a new trench had been dug in front of the fire trench. However, in places No Man's Land was so narrow that the cylinders had to be placed in the front trench. Altogether 259 bays had been dug ready for the cylinders. Lieutenant White inspected his sector on 18 September:

> *.........I reported to the brigade and inspected the emplacements on our front. These had been planned by an officer of the RE. There were 14 in all on my front, but one, being in a dangerous re-entrant, was not used. Each was intended to hold 15 cylinders. It was made by digging away the fire step and substituting a wooden platform supported by strong stakes, leaving ample room for the cylinders below it.*

Six Special Brigade sections occupied a divisional front and each section controlling about a dozen batteries. Two men, one a chemical specialist, were stationed in each emplacement, where they controlled a battery of cylinders. At the allotted times the cylinders would be opened as quickly as possible. In the gaps between smoke candles would have to be lit, and on I Corps front over 3,000 single and 700 triple candles were made available.

At First Army headquarters the weather conditions were studied intently as zero hour approached. Throughout 24 September Captain E Gold, First Army's meteorological officer, briefed General Haig on the prevailing weather conditions. A network of weather stations across northern France sent in reports on the hour, as did the Meteorological Offices in London and Paris. Messages from the gas officers at the front completed the picture. At 6.00pm Gold gave a favourable assessment for the following morning:

> *Wind southerly, changing to south-west or west, probably increasing to twenty miles an hour.*

All along the front, the roads came alive with traffic as thousands of men made their way to the front. At 1.00am the final assessment of the weather arrived from London and two hours later General Haig met his weather advisor before making his decision. Captain Gold's predictions pointed to sunrise as the favourable time for a gas release. Orders were immediately issued for the gas programme to begin at

5.50am, while the assault would begin forty minutes later:

Minutes

Zero Hour:	*Start the gas and run six cylinders one after the other at full blast until they are exhausted.*
0.12 to 0.20:	*Start the smoke. The smoke is to run concurrently with the gas if the gas is not exhausted at 0.12.*
0.20:	*Start the gas again and run six cylinders one after the other at full blast until they are all exhausted.*
0.32 to 0.40:	*Start the smoke again. The smoke is to run concurrently with the gas if the gas is not exhausted at 0.32.*
0.38:	*Turn all the gas off punctually. Thicken up smoke with triple candles.*
	Prepare for assault
0.40:	*ASSAULT*

However, General Haig was still not convinced. At 5.00am he watched from the top of the observation tower at his headquarters, Hinges chateau. The breeze was hardly noticeable, although smoke from his ADC's cigarette drifted to the north-east. Fifteen minutes later, Haig was still having second thoughts, and sent a message to I Corps headquarters asking if there was time to cancel the attack. Lieutenant-General Gough's reply showed that the moment had passed, there was no time to notify the front line troops.

At 5.50am the artillery began the final phase of the four-day barrage, meanwhile, Foulkes' men swung into action, frantically opening gas cylinders. From the observation stations a barrier of smoke and gas, ten metres high, could be seen filling the horizon. Forty minutes later, the front came alive as thousands of men climbed onto the parapet; the Battle of Loos had begun.

Message from 2nd Division Headquarters determining zero hour.

Chapter Four

2ND DIVISION'S ASSAULT

5 Brigade's attack

Brigadier-General Charles Corkran's 5 Brigade held 2nd Division's left sector, on the north bank of the La Bassée Canal. Its attack was intended to capture the German trenches between Chapelle St Roch and Canteleux, securing the Division's flank. Corkran had split his attack into two, to try and surprise the Germans. Three battalions, the 2nd Oxford & Buckinghamshire Light Infantry on the left, 1st Queen's in the centre and the 2nd Highland Light Infantry on the right, would advance at 6.00am from the trenches east of Givenchy, thirty minutes before the rest of the Division went over the top. This part of the attack would only be preceded by the first ten minutes of gas release. A mine, timed to detonate under the German front trench two minutes before zero, would hopefully stun the garrison.

5 Brigade's dispositions north of the La Bassée Canal.

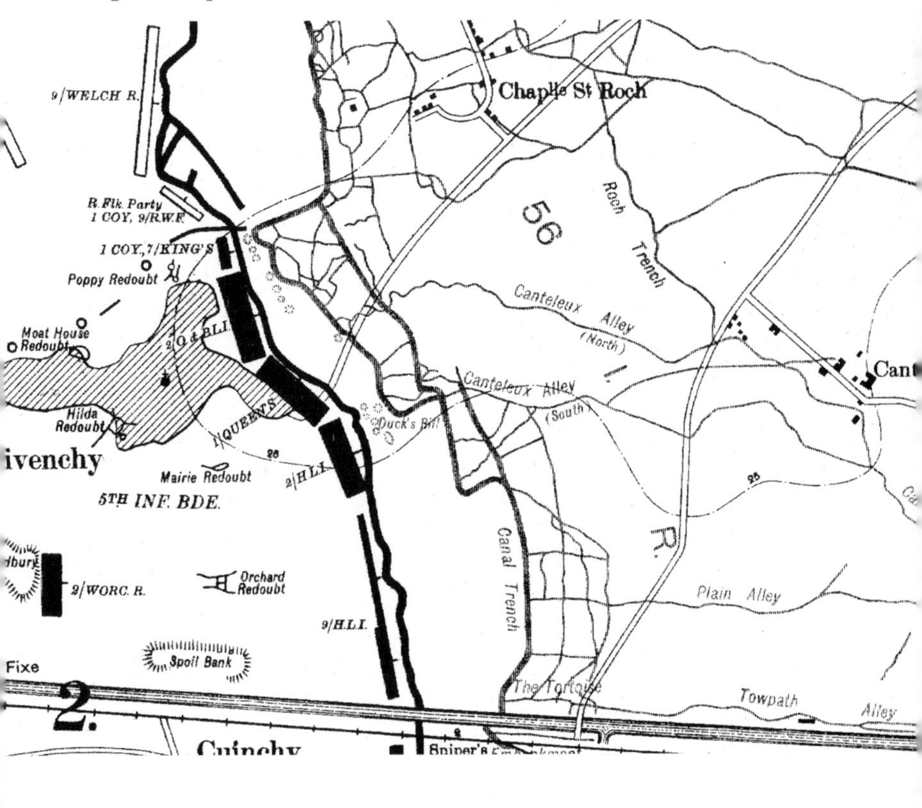

At 5.50am the gas officers began to open the taps, however, as 5 Brigade's report illustrates, it did not have the desired effect:

> *The wind was so light that the gas moved very slowly, and the enemy had time to light fires in their second line trenches, and adjust their helmets. Thus the element of surprise was absent even if the enemy had not any knowledge beforehand of our intention to use gas.*

The Ox and Bucks were badly affected by the thick clouds of gas and many were incapacitated by the poisonous fumes. At 5.58am the detonation of the mine in front of Captain Southey's D Company signalled the start of the attack. Two minutes later Southey's men left their trenches and in the words of the Battalion diarist immediately *"received a very warm reception from the enemy"*. Two parties, each with two sections, picked their way through the craters in No Man's Land, reaching the German wire. On the left, the wire was found to be intact, and the men were forced to take cover in the craters. The right hand party, under Lieutenant Pierce Newton-King, managed to find a few gaps. However, the Germans had their guns trained on them and many were killed, Newton-King included, as they tried to push forward. Meanwhile, A Company's attack was a complete success and it seemed as though the mine had destroyed all resistance. The Ox and Bucks stormed the German trench pressing on, virtually unopposed, to the support line.

In the centre, the 1st Queen's attacked with two companies; B Company under Captain Brook on the left with Major Bunbury's C

The trenches east of Givenchy, note the Duck's Bill and Tortoise Redoubt.

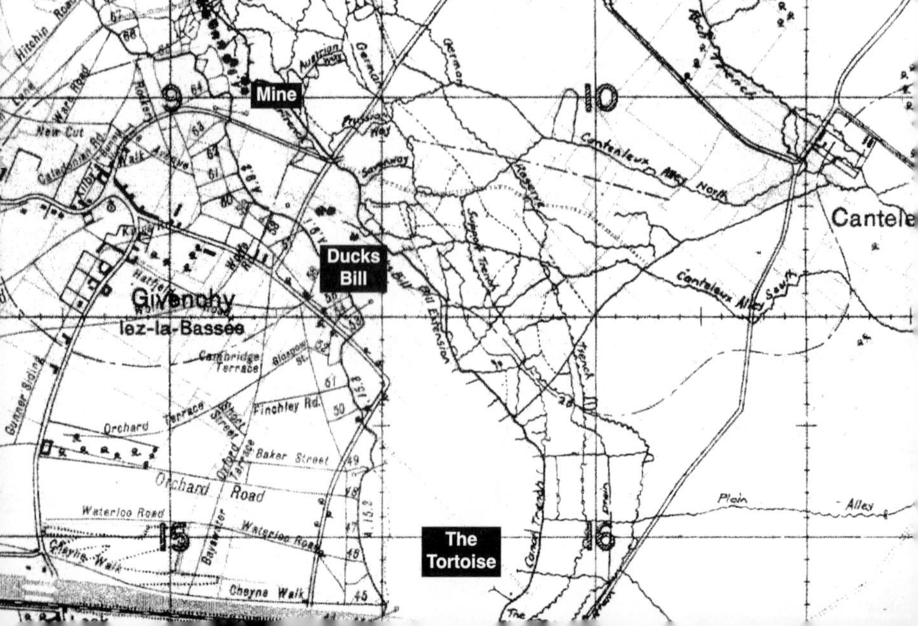

Company to their right. Yet again it appeared that the Germans had been taken by surprise and in a short space of time the fire trench had been secured. Major Bunbury was one of the few men hit crossing No Man's Land. The 2nd Highland Light Infantry were equally successful in taking their first objective. Wasting no time, the two Battalions pushed on to their next objective, the German support line. The majority advanced across the open ground, while the bombers cleared the communications trenches. The attack was going to plan; or so it seemed.

In fact when the Germans heard the mine erupting to their right, they had withdrawn fearing that their trench was also mined. As the Queen's and HLI approached the German support line they came under heavy fire. The war diary of the HLI summarises what happened next:

> *When about three quarters of the way across heavy machine gun fire was turned on them from their right... I think the Germans with machine guns and bombers were in deep dugouts somewhere along the communications trenches and came out when our leading lines were almost past them... The two leading lines closely supported by another company of the 1st Queen's meanwhile had almost reached the German second line and were in a similar manner intercepted by cross machine gun fire and forced back.*

The survivors fell back in the face of the withering fire, seeking cover in the German front line. They were at an immediate disadvantage for each battalion had only taken two hundred bombs into the German trenches, a pitiful amount to hold on for a long time. The Germans followed up along the communications trenches, probing the flanks of the Queen's and Highland Light Infantry. Meanwhile, two companies of the 1/7th King's tried to dig a communications trench across to the Duck's Bill. At 8.45am, in response to a desperate call for bombs, two platoons of the 1st Queen's, led by Lieutenant Drew, made a dash across No Man's Land. It was, however, too little too late. Those able to do so ran back across No Man's Land, braving the gauntlet of heavy machine-gun fire. Many of the wounded had to be left behind; one hundred of the 1st Queen's fell into German hands.

The second attack by 5 Brigade began at 6:30am, at the same time as the main assault south of the canal. Brigadier Corkran had hoped that the 9th (Glasgow Highland) Highland Light Infantry, a New Army battalion attached to 2nd Division, would be able to take Tortoise Reboubt. The redoubt was dug into one of the huge mounds of spoil on the canal bank. If it remained in German hands their machine-guns

No Man's Land north of the canal. Tortoise Redoubt is the embankment on the right. IWM - Q41780

could sweep the towpath and the railway embankment across the canal.

As they waited for zero hour, the leading platoons of the 9th Highland Light Infantry were engulfed in a dense cloud of gas, from across the canal. A quick role call at 6.30am revealed that only sixteen men of the two leading platoons were still fit to go on, the rest had been badly suffocated. Lieutenant-Colonel C Murray quickly ordered the support platoons forward to take their place. Ten minutes after zero the leading section emerged, to be met with a hail of bullets. Only one man returned to the fire trench. Tortoise Redoubt was obviously intact and the gas had failed to dislodge the garrison. To his credit Lieutenant-Colonel Murray called the attack off, refusing to send any more men to their deaths. By 10.00am the fighting was over on 5 Brigade's sector, and Corkran's men spent the rest of the day reorganising.

6 Brigade's attack

The centre section of 2nd Division was held by Brigadier-General Arthur Daly's 6 Brigade. Two battalions, the 2nd South Staffordshires on the left and 1st King's (Liverpool) on the right, would lead the attack, with the 1st Royal Berkshires and the 1/1st Hertfordshire Battalion following. Brigadier-General Daly had two more battalions, the 1/5th King's and 1st Kings Royal Rifle Corps, at his disposal, waiting in Cuinchy and Cambrin respectively.

Even before the hour to turn on the gas arrived, the plan began to go wrong, as described by Major Potter, the 1st King's temporary

commanding officer, in his report to brigade:

> *At 5.35am Lieutenant White* [the gas officer responsible for this sector] *reported to me that he could not use the gas as it would blow straight down our lines. Immediately afterwards the gas from the south, with dense smoke began to roll along our front line, obscuring all view and necessitating using the smoke helmets. An order was then received that the gas should be tried, and, if dangerous was to be discontinued. This was done.*

The result was a disaster, not only for 6 Brigade, but as we have already seen, for 5 Brigade across the canal. By the time zero hour arrived the

2nd Division's dispositions south of the La Bassée Canal.

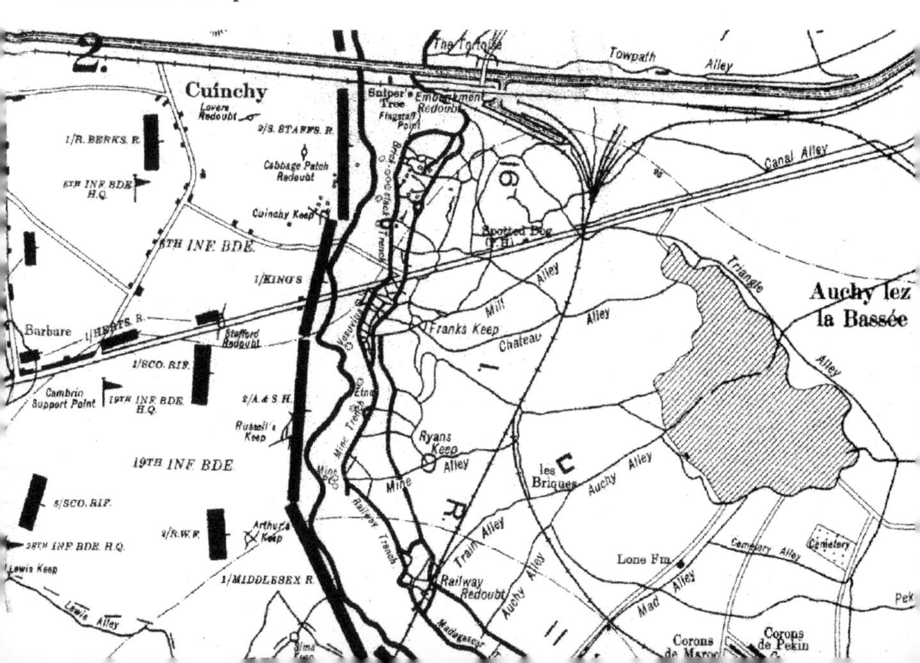

Aerial photo of the Canal sector, the brickyard south of the canal is clearly visible. IWM - Q44785

gas had ruined any chance of an effective attack being made;

......many were so badly gassed as to be incapable of advancing, whilst all suffered more or less.

It appears that the light wind had carried the noxious clouds north along the front of 2nd Division, where it settled along the canal bank, smothering the Staffordshires. To make matters worse, activity could be seen in the trenches across No Man's Land, and it was obvious that the gas had not affected the Germans. All along their front line fires sprang up on the parapet. They were lit to form a wall of warm air in the hope of lifting the gas over the trenches.

At 6.30am Captain Arthur Kilby led C Company along the canal towpath. Ahead stood Embankment Redoubt, a formidable obstacle built into the raised railway embankment. From their elevated position the German machine-guns dominated both sides of the canal. As Kilby's men advanced they came under heavy fire, not only from the Embankment, but from Tortoise Redoubt across the canal, where 5 Brigade had called off its attack. Kilby was hit in the hand almost at once but he continued to lead his diminishing group as far as the undamaged wire. Some tried to cut a way through, while others tried

Captain Arthur Kilby VC.

to throw bombs into the German trenches. Captain Kilby was seriously wounded, losing his foot to one bomb explosion. He still fought on encouraging his men and firing his rifle. Second Lieutenant D M Williams attempted to support the attack by bringing his machine-gun team forward. From a position on the railway embankment the machine-gun helped to subdue the redoubt for a time.

At 8.00am the order to withdraw was given, bringing the attempt to capture Embankment Redoubt to an end. Only two of Williams' team returned. When darkness fell several of Kilby's men made an unsuccessful search for their officer's body. Captain Arthur Kilby was posthumously awarded the Victoria Cross for leading the attack on the redoubt. He was originally remembered on the Dud Corner Memorial to the Missing along with his men. Excavation work did, however, uncover his body in February 1929. His remains were interred at Arras Road Cemetery, Roclincourt, many miles to the south.

A and B Companies faced the infamous Brickstacks sector. No Man's Land was extremely narrow, winding its way between stacks of bricks, each one fortified and concealing a dugout. For over six months 170th Tunnelling Company had been waging an underground war with the German miners and by September a necklace of craters filled No Man's Land. The Staffords would have to thread their way through the gaps to reach the German trenches.

The Brickstacks. Each stack concealed a manned dugout. IWM - Q41775

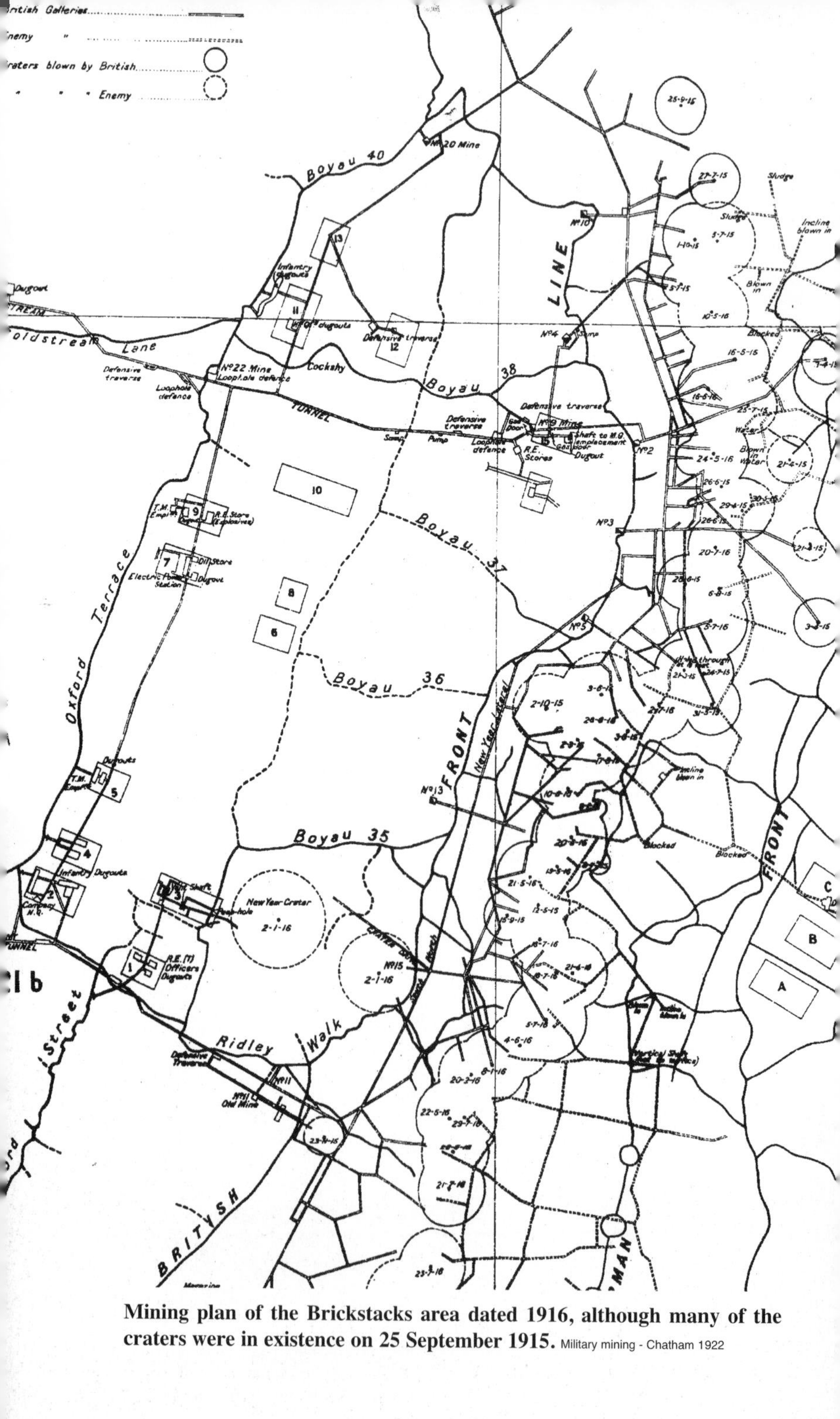

Mining plan of the Brickstacks area dated 1916, although many of the craters were in existence on 25 September 1915. Military mining - Chatham 1922

Yet again, many of the assault troops had been asphyxiated before zero hour. Two minutes before zero two small mines, designed to stun the Germans, detonated under their front line. They had little effect; in anticipation of a mine attack the garrison had withdrawn to their support line, returning immediately after the explosions. The Staffordshires' war diary details A and B Companies brave attempt:

> *As the signal for the assault was given, our men rushed gallantly forward, only to be met by cross-fire from concealed machine-guns and heavy rifle fire from the German front-line trench, the enemy evidently being quite unaffected by the gas. 'A' and 'B' Companies were held up on the craters nearest to their parapet and were unable to advance.*

The 1st King's, commanded by Lieutenant-Colonel H Potter, held the right hand sector of the Brigade, astride the La Basseé Road. This time it was the dense smoke-screen that doomed the attack to failure. Potter's report to brigade headquarters describes how the attack faltered:

> *Punctually at 6.30am the leading platoons on both sides of the road jumped over the parapet and advanced. That on the south side of the road was immediately wiped out by machine-gun fire and no further advance was attempted, as the wire was not broken. On the north side all the platoons of 'B' Company advanced and soon reached the enemy's wire. In the dense smoke which blew along the front line the leading platoon went a little too much to the right and some men crossed the road.*

Lieutenant-Colonel Potter could not see the disaster that had befallen his men through the smoke. Fortunately, Lieutenant (acting Captain) James Ryan braved the machine-gun fire and ran back to report the bad

No Man's Land south of the La Bassée road. IWM - Q41768

news. Lieutenant-Colonel Potter, acting on Ryan's information, suspended further attacks:

I then held up the attack as the gas had failed us and a further advance for the time being appeared to be only a sacrifice of life.

Lieutenant Ryan returned to his men, disappearing though the smoke, never to be seen again. His name is carved on the panels of Dud Corner Memorial.

In a little over an hour 6 Brigade's attack was over. Further attempts were planned at Divisional level, but they came to nothing. Subsequent artillery bombardments failed to make an impression on the German wire.

19 Brigade

The right sector of 2nd Division was held by Brigadier-General Philip Robertson's 19 Brigade. The 2nd Argyll & Sutherland Highlanders and 1st Middlesex would lead the assault, with the 1st Scottish Rifles and the 2nd Royal Welch Fusiliers following. The strip of land faced by Roberston's men was fraught with difficulties. Tunnelling teams had been fighting a war underground for the past twelve months and a ribbon of mine craters filled No Man's Land. In

The formidable trench system protecting Auchy-lès-Mines.

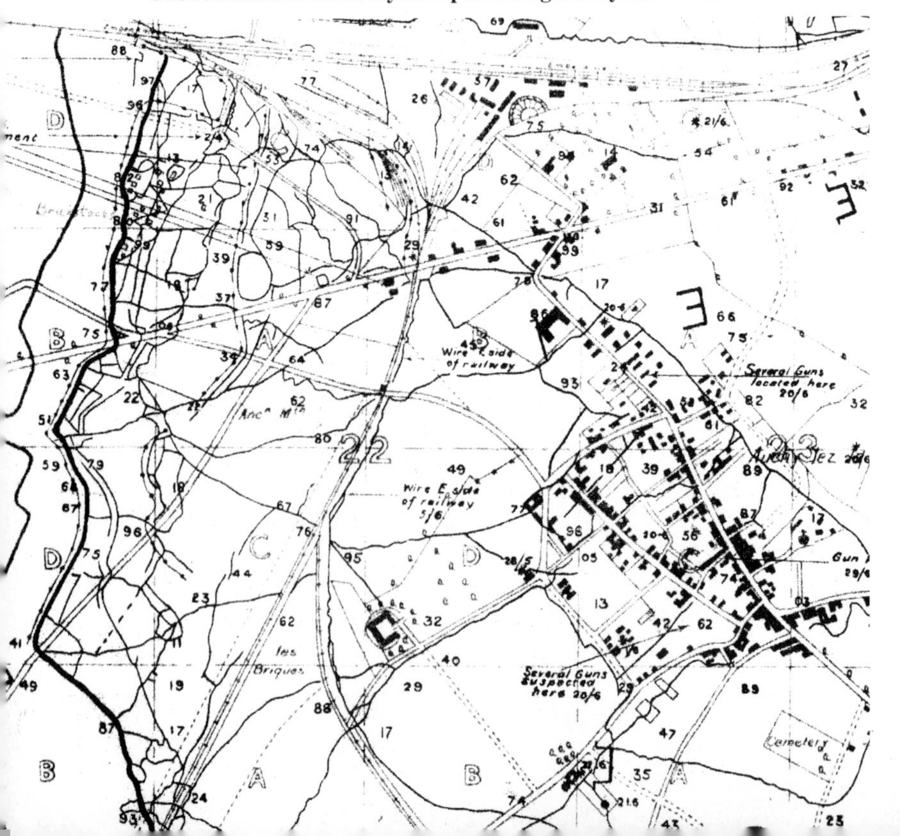

places the British held one lip while the Germans held the other. The amount of debris created by a detonated mine was enormous and many craters were surrounded by rims of earth over two metres high. The artillery's wire cutting operation was severely hampered by these obstacles and in some areas it had been impossible to wreck the wire. German wiring parties usually repaired any damage under the cover of darkness. Twenty-four hours before zero Lieutenant-Colonel Rowley, the Middlesex's commanding officer, reported that the wire on his sector had suffered little damage and his patrols estimated that the entanglement was up to twenty-five metres wide in places.

The craters had also made it difficult to prepare a system of assembly trenches. No Man's Land was so narrow that it had been impossible to dig a trench for the gas cylinders. In places the jumping off trench was fifty metres behind the original fire trench. The assault troops would be exposed to German machine-guns for longer than desirable. The war diary of the 2nd Argylls gives a detailed description of the plan:

During the night the wire in front of our 'jumping off' trenches was removed and trenches were bridged about 30 to 40 yards in rear of the fire trench..... Forty short scaling ladders were in position in each trench. Two companies had two platoons formed up in these 'jumping off' trenches, one standing at the ladders the other platoon standing beside the ladders, the two other platoons of these companies were formed up in the support trenches known as High Street. It was hoped that four waves of troops would emerge almost simultaneously, taking the Germans by surprise.

Two future authors were present during 19 Brigade's attack, serving with the 2nd Royal Welch Fusiliers. Lieutenant Robert Graves recalled his experiences in his autobiography *Goodbye to All That*, while Frank Richards gives a private's view of events in his memoirs *Old Soldiers Never Die*. Both accounts convey the feeling of pessimism felt by all ranks in the days leading up to the attack. Above all there was a distrust of the Special Brigade and their dreaded cylinders. In the words of one of Richards' comrades:

.... If this attack does come off on this particular part of the front it's going to be the biggest balls-up ever known, and unless 'J.C.' is very kind to us the majority of the Brigade will be skinned alive.

As zero hour approached, the weather turned against the Special Brigade, prompting Captain Percy-Smith, the gas officer in charge of

19 Brigade's view of Auchy. Chalk thrown up by two huge mines can be seen on the left. IWM - Q41770

the sector, to report to Divisional headquarters:

Dead calm. Impossible to discharge accessory.

His advice was overruled and the reply called for the gas programme to be followed in spite of the weather. Lieutenant-Colonel Rowley's report illustrates how the gas failed to affect the Germans:

The gas poured forth in great volume. But owing to lack of wind, it moved very slowly, and appeared to drift obliquely between the two lines, and to grow very thin, as it approached the hostile trenches.

Two minutes before zero hour two mines detonated beneath the German front line. It had been hoped that they would sufficiently disrupt the garrison, allowing the assault troops to take them by surprise. As we have seen, the premature attack north of the canal had thoroughly alerted the Germans. Fearing a mine attack many had evacuated their trench, returning as soon as the debris settled. As the minutes ticked by, observers saw heads and rifles appearing over the parapet eighty metres away, it appeared that the gas had done nothing to deter the Germans.

At zero hour the whistles blew and the leading platoons climbed out of their trenches. Due to the number of mine craters the Battalion's frontage was limited to a single gap, sixty metres wide. With the Highlanders forced to bunch together, the Germans could hardy fail to miss. 16 Platoon bore the brunt of the German guns and Lieutenant John Bullough, along with most of his platoon, was killed as they crossed the German wire. 5 Platoon, following behind, also braved the bullets to reach their first objective. Lieutenant Alexander Gillespie, the platoon commander, was shot dead as he leapt over the German parapet. Only ten men, under Sergeant Angus McClure, managed to enter the German trenches.

Machine-guns on the flanks of the attack were now trained on the gap between the craters. Lieutenant MacPherson brought the Battalion machine-guns into action, in the hope of supporting a renewed advance. His efforts were in vain. With the forward trenches congested with wounded, A Company was forced to advance from the support trenches. Valiant attempts were made to move forward, but most were shot down before they had crossed the original fire trench. The Battalion diary describes how the Argylls suffered:

> *One more platoon of 'B' Company succeeded in crossing the fire trench but were unable to reach the German trenches and support the leading platoon. Owing to the heaviness of the fire the remaining platoons were unable to cross the fire trench. 'A' Company endeavoured to cross but were unable to make any headway.*

The disaster cost the Argylls' dearly, over three hundred were killed or wounded. Sergeant McClure was killed and his isolated party was taken captive.

No Man's Land on the Middlesex sector posed a different problem

19 Brigade's assembly trenches detailing supply dumps.

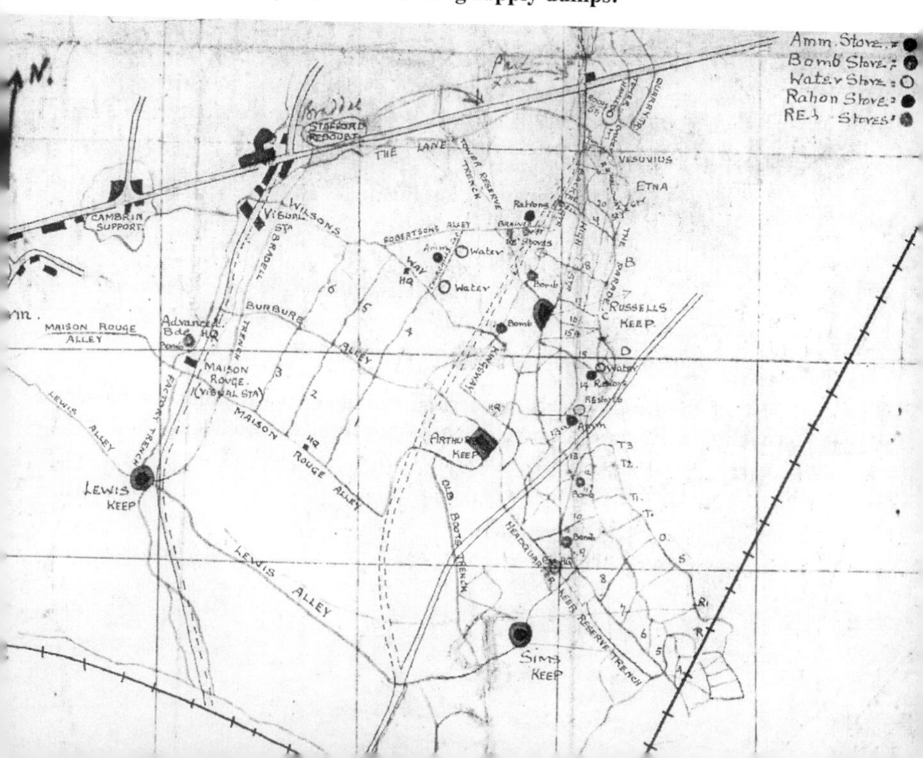

for Lieutenant-Colonel Rowley's men. The craters were rather more scattered, but nonetheless proved a serious obstacle. It was impossible for the assault troops to advance in waves. The heavily laden men would have to pick their way between the craters.

At 6.30am 'A', 'B' and 'C' Companies emerged simultaneously from their assembly trenches. With the Germans fully alerted, the Middlesex men made easy targets and they were greeted by a murderous fire from machine-guns and rifles. Many Germans felt so confident that they stood on the parapet to take aim. Few made it more than a few yards before they were struck down. Seeing the attack falter, Lieutenant-Colonel Rowley ordered 3 platoons of his reserve company forward to try and rally the stricken men. They too met the same fate.

Just before 7.00am Brigadier-General Roberston sent a message to Lieutenant-Colonel Rowley asking for information:

> *Any news? How far have you advanced. Is gas returning you. Keep me well informed so that artillery barrage may be altered to suit if you want it.*

Brigade headquarters did not have to wait for long. Over the next half-hour the awful truth unfolded in a series of messages:

6.50am: Much opposition to our front. Please ask guns to shell Le Briques trench.

7.00am: Reserve company has got on, but we are being heavily fired on.

7.16am: Line held up. Very heavy fire.

7.20am: Ask guns to shell German front line trench. Railway Trench I mean.

With no more reserves to call on Lieutenant-Colonel Rowley requested support from the 2nd Royal Welch Fusiliers. Both Robert Graves and Frank Richards had waited in the Fusiliers' support trenches, listening to the battle unfold a hundred metres away.

> *All we heard back there was a distant cheer, confused crackle of rifle fire, yells, heavy shelling on our front line, more shells and yells and a continuous rattle of machine-guns.*

Men of the Royal Welch Fusiliers march along the Bethune-La Bassée road to the village of Cambrin, where they awaited zero hour.

German view of No Man's Land. IWM - Q28979

Minutes later lightly wounded men came stumbling down the trenches, followed by the gassed; their faces yellow. Frank Richards' asked one what had happened; *'a bloody balls up'* was the colourful but honest reply. By the time Rowley's request for reinforcements arrived, the communication trenches were over-flowing with wounded. It took 'B' and 'C' Companies of the Welch thirty minutes to get into position. Some platoons lost their way as they tried to find a way through. Meanwhile Lieutenant-Colonel Rowley continued to pass a series of confusing messages to brigade headquarters:

7.26am: Don't think gas is affecting us or Germans. They are holding their front line trench. Our Battalion is all out in area between their front trench and ours. 2nd Royal Welsh Fusiliers are now up. It is essential to now shell hostile front trench.

7.30am: Reported casualties now 400, but impossible to tell. Have observed enormous number fall.

7.55am: Must shell German first line. Our men are all out in front. Almost all must be killed or wounded. Please shell first line. Welch Fusiliers are now advancing.

As soon as the Royal Welch Fusiliers clambered over the parapet, machine-guns swept them away, relentlessly traversing backwards and forwards. In a matter of minutes the attack was over. One officer told Robert Graves what happened to his platoon:

It had been agreed to advance by platoon rushes with supporting fire. When his platoon had run about twenty yards he signalled them to lie down and open covering fire. The din was tremendous. He saw the platoon on the left flopping down too, so he whistled the advance again. Nobody seemed to hear. He jumped up from his shell-hole and waved and signalled 'Forward'. Nobody stirred. He shouted 'You bloody cowards, are you leaving me to go alone?' His platoon sergeant, groaning with a broken shoulder, gasped out: 'Not cowards Sir. Willing enough. But they are all f...... dead'. A machine gun traversing had caught them as they rose to the whistle.

By 8.00am it was over. Desperate messages from No Man's Land called for reinforcements, but there were none available. A message from Lieutenant A D Hill, stranded in No Man's Land, reported that:

Enemy very strong in front with machine-guns and rifles. 'C' Company only about 30 or 35 men. Impossible to advance on account of machine-guns. Mr Henry and three men alone remain out of two platoons. Can we have reinforcements?

Another message from Second Lieutenant P Choate told the same story:

'B' Company attack held up 100 yards out of our trench. Major Swainson wounded. 'B' Company knocked out, few men stand fast.

Lieutenant-Colonel Rowley could not afford to send any more men over the top. He needed every man available to hold the fire trench, in case the Germans counter-attacked.

The only success occurred on the Battalion's left flank. The grenade reserve platoon, supported by the fourth platoon of 'D' Company had managed to enter 'D' Point craters close to the German trenches. One of the battalion's machine-gun teams succeeded in joining the group later on. From the advanced position they were able to suppress the Germans for the rest of the day, allowing many British troops to escape No Man's Land.

Major-General Horne wanted to renew the attack south of the canal and at 9.00am he ordered a thirty minute barrage of the German positions. Brigadier-General Daly objected to the order to attack with the support battalions;

The gas was a complete failure against the enemy, but our men suffered very heavy casualties and are not in a position to attack again

All the battalion commanders concerned protested, and for once sense prevailed. At 9.45am Major-General Horne called off the attack, but for many men it was only the start of a long, agonising day. With little cover in No Man's Land, they were forced to hide where they could until darkness fell. Any sign of movement attracted a stream of bullets. The attack on Railway Trench had cost the Middlesex dearly, sixteen officers and 436 men. The two Royal Welch companies suffered over one hundred casualties.

Chapter Five

9TH (SCOTTISH) DIVISION

28 Brigade's attack

Brigadier-General Spencer ScraseDickins' 28 Brigade held the left-hand sector of the 9th (Scottish) Division. The Brigade had encountered a number of difficulties prior to the day of the attack. A few days earlier I Corps had ordered a reorganisation of its front, calling for an extension to 2nd Division's front. This had left 28 Brigade in a cramped position, with only one communications trench to cater for both the reinforcements and the wounded. It was a problem that would hamper movement in this sector throughout the forthcoming battle. To make matters worse it appears that no patrols were sent out at night to report on the effectiveness of the wire-cutting operation. Without accurate information to rely on, the artillery had been firing blind. It was an oversight that would cost the Scots dearly.

The left of the Brigade, held by the 10th Highland Light Infantry, faced Madagascar Trench. Two strong points flanked the HLI's front, Railway Redoubt to their left and Mad Point on the right. Mad Point extended forward from the German trenches and its machine guns would be able to sweep across the full frontage of the Brigade as the

9th (Scottish) Division's dispositions at zero hour.

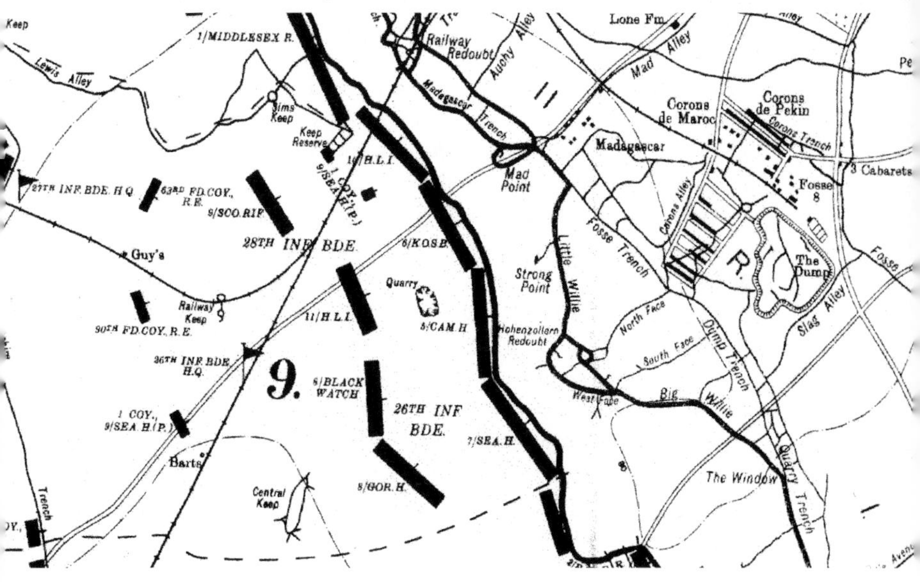

men crossed No Man's Land. The 6th Kings Own Scottish Borderers (KOSB's), on the right of the Brigade front, faced Little Willie Trench. A sap to the KOSB's right ended in a concrete emplacement, known simply as Strongpoint. It was ideally placed to fire into the KOSB's flank as soon as they left their trenches. The 9th Scottish Rifles (Cameronians) and the 11th Highland Light Infantry were in support, to the left and right respectively.

The gas release started well, but as the minutes ticked, problems began to mount. German artillery began shelling the crowded trenches as soon as the gas cloud appeared. The shrapnel caused many casualties in the crowded assembly trenches, including Lieutenant-Colonel H D N MacLean, the 6th KOSB's commanding officer. It also managed to shatter a number of gas cylinders, spraying the assault troops with concentrated chlorine gas. The wind proved insufficient to carry the gas across No Man's Land and, as zero hour approached, it drifted back over the Scottish trenches. Many of the Scots were put out of action, including Lieutenant-Colonel J C Grahame, the CO of the 10th Highland Light Infantry.

In spite of these of problems, the 10th Highland Light Infantry advanced on time. As soon as the men climbed over the parapet it became obvious that both Railway Redoubt and Mad Point were active. As the Battalion diary reports, the crossfire was devastating:

> *The attack was launched; all the lines rose out of the trenches simultaneously, and advanced under a very heavy machine-gun, rifle and shell fire. The first line were practically wiped out before they had gone 20 yards, the 2nd and 3rd lines lost very heavily before they reached our own 1st line. By the time all the three first companies were over we had lost 70% of the men who went over and about 85% of the officers. C Company advanced about quarter of an hour afterwards and also lost very heavily.*

To make matters worse a shell destroyed the headquarters dugout, cutting the communication link with brigade headquarters. Lieutenant-Colonel A C Northey, CO of the 9th Scottish Rifles, went forward just after zero hour to assess the situation before he ordered his men forward. He found the front line trenches in a state of utter chaos:

> *... there was considerable confusion everywhere and a strong smell of gas, the latter being in my opinion from shells and not from our own cylinders. From this moment it became increasingly difficult to obtain any information as to what was happening. I heard that Lt.-Col. Grahame had been gassed and found him in the old support trench, he was almost incoherent*

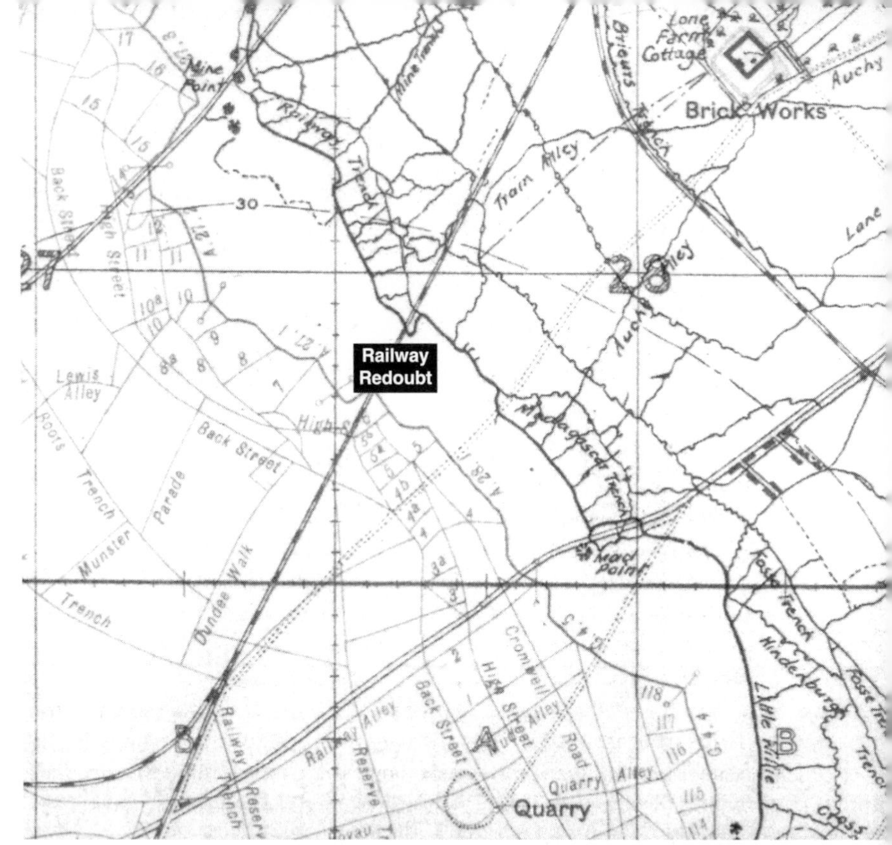

Trench map covering the areas around Railway Redoubt and Mad Point.

and I could gather nothing from him. His orderly, who was with him, stated that the 10th had gained the German Line and were occupying their first three lines of trenches. I am under the impression that the liaison officer was present at the moment and passed this information to the brigade.

Brigadier ScraseDickins was to be influenced by this inaccurate piece of information for several hours.

On the right of the Brigade front the 6th KOSB climbed out of their trenches at 6.30am, amidst thick clouds of gas. At first the leading platoons were unable to see and their officers instructed the men to lie down in front of the parapet in the hope that the gas might disperse. The support companies meanwhile, emerged from their trenches and at once came under fire from Mad Point. In their haste to push on they caught up with the leading wave and the whole Battalion began to move forward as one. The guns in Mad Point could not fail to miss the dense target and the KOSB lost heavily. Major William Hosley, the second in command, was one of the first casualties, wounded as he

Although damaged by the four day barrage, the wire was impassable in many places. IWM - Q28969

climbed on to the parapet. He refused to return to have his wounds tended, remaining for some time at his post directing operations. Hosley died soon afterwards at the dressing station in Cambrin. Pipe-Major Robert Mackenzie was struck down as he piped the men forward. He died of his wounds on 8 October at Etaples Base Hospital near Boulogne. At fifty-nine years old he was one of the oldest casualties at Loos.

As the men advanced the machine-gun in the Strongpoint began firing into the Scots' right flank at close range. There were many casualties, but the KOSBs pushed on towards Little Willie Trench and, with only a few yards to go, they broke into a run. To their horror the men fell, literally, into an ingenious trap. The Germans had dug a ditch filled with barbed wire and stakes to protect their fire trench. Netting, supporting a layer of turf, camouflaged the ditch until the last moment. Those with wire-cutters set to work trying to cut a way through, while the rest looked on helpless. When Mad Point finished dealing with the 10th Highland Light Infantry, it turned its attention on the KOSB:

The position was reached and at some point entered. Severe machine-gun fire, chiefly from the flanks, undestroyed obstacles and uncertain effects of gas caused severe casualties and prevented the attack from succeeding. In a matter of minutes the Battalion was destroyed, all but one officer and over six hundred men were killed or wounded in the death trap. Only Lieutenant W N Watson remained unscathed and endeavoured to form a firing line in the hope that reinforcements arrived soon.

The survivors were trapped, the wire-filled ditch blocked the way forward while machine-guns swept the ground behind. The regimental history laments how:

The wonderful product of months of zeal, energy and patriotism was knocked out without opportunity of doing more than set an example to posterity by their bravery.

For several hours nothing was heard of the disaster in front of Little Willie Trench. As far as Brigade knew, the attack was going to plan. In reality it was a fiasco. The assault battalions had been all but wiped out and the supports were still struggling to get into position through the congested trenches. In the confusion some men over-reacted to the stench of gas permeating the trenches.

It had taken the Scottish Rifles over an hour to get into position opposite Railway Trench on the left of the Brigade front. One company had been ordered to retire by a panicked officer as it made its way forward along Reid's Alley. At 8.00am Lieutenant-Colonel Northey received the first indication that the HLI had failed to cross No Man's Land:

I was handed a message which Major Stewart 10th HLI had managed to get in from in front on the right, stating that he was hung up on that flank, half his company practically non-existent, and urgently required support.

After sending the information on to Brigade headquarters, Northey decided personally to go forward into the front trench to assess the situation. What he discovered there was disturbing:

The enemy appeared to be in undisturbed possession of their front line, and in my opinion there was not a man of the attacking battalion in front of our parapet except the dead and wounded.

At 9.30am instructions arrived from Brigade instructing two companies of the Scottish Rifles to move forward in support of the 10th Highland Light Infantry. It was obvious to Lieutenant-Colonel Northey that Brigade headquarters were acting in ignorance of the facts. He did not want to send men to certain death and disregarded the order, making sure his men stood their ground before sending a second report to Brigade. For over two hours nothing was heard and for the time being it seemed that Brigade had seen sense.

On the right, the 11th Highland Light Infantry had also found it impossible to move forward into the cramped assembly trenches against the flow of wounded men. The stench of gas everywhere only added to the troops' discomfort. Having heard nothing of the KOSBs, Lieutenant-Colonel Fergusson watched and waited until 9.30am, when the first message came in from the from the Borderers:

Now retiring. Cannot go further unless reinforcements sent.

Lieutenant-Colonel Fergusson immediately sent Major C E Andrews with two companies over the top in support. The machine guns in Mad Point and Strongpoint made short work of them in a matter of minutes.

Half an hour later an order from Brigade headquarters arrived. Its contents illustrate just how misinformed Brigadier-General Scrase-Dickins was:

Send two companies in support to German support trench. Second Division still fighting about LES BRIQUES. Be prepared to help making defensive flank to me along BRIQUES trench.

Having pre-empted the Brigade's order, Lieutenant-Colonel Fergusson decided to hold the rest of his men in the assembly trenches and wait for further developments. He notified Brigade of his position and made it clear that he would not send his remaining companies forward unless ordered to do so. So far he had heard nothing more from the KOSB or his own men and did not know if anyone had entered Little Willie Trench. In fact, Fergusson heard nothing else for over two hours, either from in front or from Brigade. The silence was ominous.

26 Brigade's attack

The right sector of 9th Division faced one of the most unenviable tasks on 25 September 1915. Its first task was to capture Hohenzollen Redoubt, the large defensive entrenchment overlooking No Man's Land. The next objective included the Fosse 8 mining complex, where the Scots would have to clear the miners houses (or Corons) and pithead buildings. The right of the Brigade faced the Dump and its dugouts.

Brigadier-General Archibald Ritchie deployed his battalions in accordance with the patterning of their glengarries; dark patterns to the left, and diced patterns to the right. The 5th Cameron Highlanders, led by Lieutenant-Colonel Cameron of Lochiel, would lead the attack against Little Willie Trench, north of the redoubt. As the Cameron's made their way through the Corons, the 8th Black Watch would follow in support. The task of taking the redoubt itself fell to the 7th Seaforth Highlanders, with the 8th Gordon Highlanders in support.

A diagram to show 9th Division's objectives.

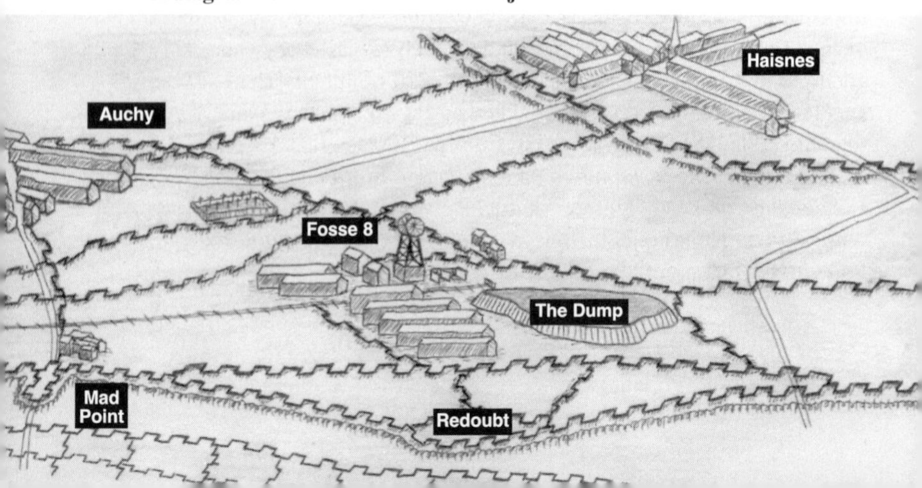

Scots take a break while their comrade fires a signal flare.

On this front, more than any other, the smoke screen had to conceal the advance. Phosphorous grenades would be used to supplement the usual smoke candles, while a battery of Stokes Mortars (in use as smoke projectors for the first time) provided a covering barrage of smoke shells. It had been impossible to dig new assembly trenches close to the redoubt, and engineers had supervised the digging of shallow tunnels (known as Russian saps) across No Man's Land. As darkness fell on the 24th, the Scots opened out the tunnels and dug shallow assembly trenches. Although this approach ensured the element of surprise in the opening minutes, it meant that the support troops would be hampered by the lack of properly formed trenches.

With zero approaching, the smoke screen allowed the men to move out beyond their wire and form up unnoticed. On the Cameron's front it was, however, a severe hindrance. Hampered by their smoke helmets, the assault troops became disorientated; officers were unable to find their men and few knew which direction the German trenches were. It took ten minutes to reorganise, by which time many had collapsed, badly suffocated by gas.

While the Cameron Highlanders tried to form up, the 7th Seaforth Highlanders moved forward on time. It is necessary to follow the Seaforth's progress first to understand how the Brigade's advance developed. The smoke assisted Lieutenant-Colonel Walter Gaisford's men and for once the assault troops made good progress, as reported in the battalion diary:

> *... at 6.29am the troops got out of the trench and formed up behind the smoke barrier. They advanced at 6.30am at a steady walk and, after having got a little distance, machine-gun and rifle fire was spewed on us. This was not very accurate as the smoke, behind which we advanced, rendered it difficult for the Germans to see us clearly. A few men went down under this fire, which seemed to come from machine-guns to our right. The Germans were holding the Redoubt and we lost a good many officers in the Redoubt's First Trench.*

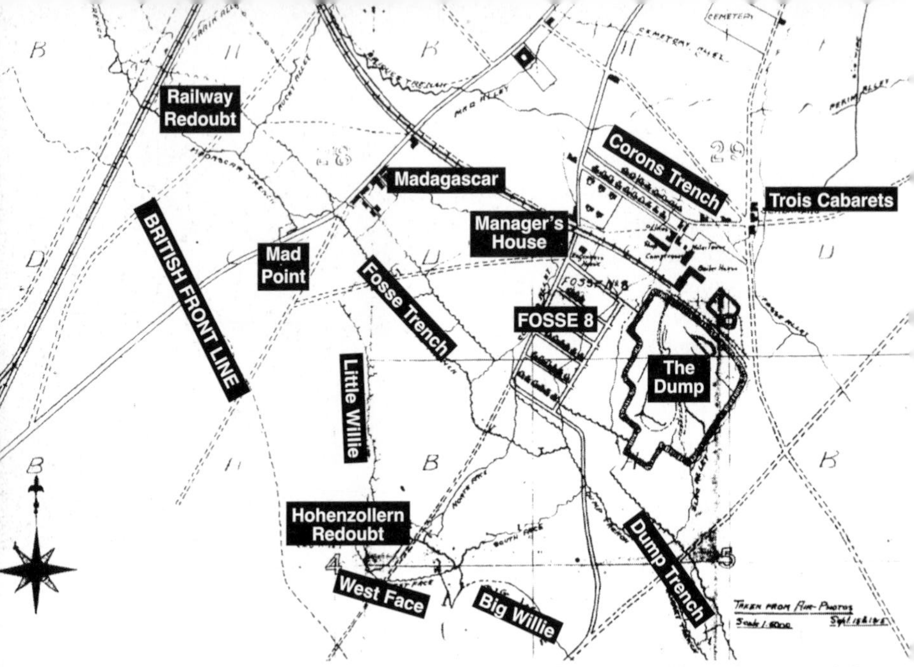

Plan of Fosse 8 and Hohenzollern Redoubt taken from aerial photographs, 15 September.

The machine-guns referred to were stationed in Big Willie Trench, which extends east from the redoubt. Due to the divergent attacks of 9th and 7th Divisions, this section of trench was not engaged during the initial assault.

Having cleared West Face Trench, the Battalion bombers entered the maze of trenches and began clearing dugouts. Meanwhile, the infantry pushed on over the top towards Dump Trench and Fosse 8. The Battalion diary glosses over the spectacular advance:

> *We continued to advance and bombed up the communications trenches from Hohenzollen to the main German trench. On our left we made good the miners' cottages, but the Camerons, whose business it was to keep touch with us, for some reason lost touch and we had to make good all these cottages. The orders which we had previously received, being to press on and not to wait ....*

Although they were unsupported on either flank, the Seaforth's pushed on relentlessly. Resistance on their own front was light and it seemed as though many Germans had fled. Beyond Dump Trench the Seaforths entered the Corons, five rows of miners cottages. As they began clearing them, heavy machine-gun fire from Madagascar and Lone Farm to the west began sweeping through the streets, causing heavy casualties.

By 7.30am the Seaforths had reached the northern edge of Fosse 8

Artist's impression of the attack.

and began to consolidate Corons Trench, which skirted the mine buildings. The work was complicated by the fact that the Germans had flooded the trench before they left. Having taken all their objectives, the Seaforths waited for the supports. In little over an hour they had advanced a mile, clearing some of the most difficult terrain on the battlefield. Although the advance had been a complete success, over half the battalion lay dead or wounded. Officer casualties were particularly severe, and only a handful survived to organise the defence of the colliery.

We had left the 5th Cameron Highlanders in front of their trenches, shrouded in a thick cloud of smoke. After a delay of ten minutes, Lieutenant-Colonel Cameron of Lochiel ordered his men forward. Pushing on, the Camerons crossed Little Willie Trench and headed for Fosse Trench. However, as soon as A and B companies emerged from the smoke screen, Mad Point spotted the tempting target and opened fire. Before the Battalion reached the Corons it had lost over half its number, as reported in the war diary:

> *It was found that the whole line of advance was enfiladed by heavy machine-gun and rifle fire from MAD PT. and MADAGASCAR. This fire had caused us very heavy losses, practically having wiped out the first two lines. With HQ the remains of 'D' and the other lines pushed forward and reached SW corner of the CORONS.*

The survivors headed into the Corons and by using the buildings as cover they moved quickly forward. With wounded Highlanders cheering the Camerons as they advanced, it was obvious that the Seaforths had already passed through:

It was found on our arrival at the forward end of the CORONS that the 7th SEAFORTH had already gained their objective. They had not been subjected to the same enfilade fire from the left. Some 25 of our A Coy were also in position near the THREE CABARETS on the left of 7th SEAFORTH.

Lord Lochiel immediately sought out Lieutenant-Colonel Gaisford and the two decided to hold their ground. There was no sign of progress to the left, where 28 Brigade should have been, and enfilading fire from that direction continued to cause casualties. While the Seaforths continued to work on Corons Trench, the Camerons formed a protective flank across the railway line to their left, to guard against counterattacks from Madagascar. The two COs set up their headquarters in the mine manager's house on the extreme left flank.

Meanwhile the 8th Black Watch, who had waited in the rear of the 5th Camerons, were moving forward towards the Corons:

Heavy enemy artillery fire had by this time been directed on our front line trench and the ground immediately in front of it, which caused considerable casualties. The enemy trench LITTLE WILLIE and the ground immediately in front of it was swept with a very heavy machine-gun fire from the direction of MADAGASCAR and MAD POINT which was seriously diminishing the ranks of the advancing lines. Low wire entanglements were here much in evidence in order to check the pace of the advancing lines and an enfilade fire from the left, i.e. MADAGASCAR, told heavily.

As they crossed Little Willie Trench, the Black Watch became hidden behind the contours of the ground. With no other target to focus on, the Mad Point guns swung round to wait for the Scots to emerge as they headed for the Corons. In instances like these the insistence on a swift advance over the top, rather than allowing the men to take the slower but safer route along German trenches, would cost the Black Watch dearly.

When DUMP TRENCH was reached little or no hostile fire was met with till we neared the east end of the CORONS when heavy machine-gun fire from the north, i.e. junction of MAD ALLEY and the railway, was brought to bear on us, sweeping from the railway and the roads between the houses of the CORONS. Also, serious fire was brought to bear on us from the direction of HAISNES on our right and the junction of BRIQUES TRENCH and MAD ALLEY. When we reached the road running

Panorama of Fosse 8 and the Dump. Detail from IWM - Q37764 and IWM Q37765

along the west side of the most eastern row of houses a very heavy machine-gun, rifle and shrapnel fire was directed on us, especially from MAD ALLEY and LONE FARM, at this point we lost very heavily. Passing this road and going into the trench running round the east side of the CORONS we halted temporarily ...

Only two hundred and fifty Black Watch reached the forward position in Fosse 8, bringing the total strength of the force in Fosse 8 to little over seven hundred. Their precarious position is described in the 5th Cameron's diary:

By this time the only officers of the battalion remaining were the CO and adjutant and there were about 80 NCOs and men. These, with the Black Watch, combined and formed a mixed force of some 300 odd men, who held part of the forward end of the CORONS in a trench (with the 7th SEAFORTH on the right) and part of our left flank. A small party watched our flank at the railway crossing and this flank, was subsequently extended further towards FOSSE TRENCH. Our line of defence, on the front part of our left flank was an 18 inch thick brick wall, then from the MANAGER'S HOUSE along CORONS TRENCH ..... Our left flank was really in the air, as the Germans were still holding their main line west of MADAGASCAR. But our machine-guns (two) had remained in LITTLE WILLIE and thus protected this flank to a considerable extent.

Lieutenant-Colonel Lochiel, the only battalion commander still standing, did his best to steady his men. With no sign of reinforcements he worked hard to maintain his dwindling command. It began to look as though 28 Brigade had failed to make any progress at all, which left Lochiel in an exposed position. To make matters worse there was no sign of activity to the north, where 2nd Division should have been moving into Auchy-lès-Mines.

The final battalion of 26 Brigade, the 8th Gordon Highlanders, moved in close support of the Seaforths. As they crossed Hohenzollen Redoubt, a quick search of the trenches and dugouts uncovered forty prisoners. Lieutenant-Colonel Wright's men managed to reach Dump Trench without attracting attention and waited there for further instructions. An hour later he was notified that the rest of the Brigade was moving through Fosse 8 and it appeared as though the attack was going to plan. Lieutenant-Colonel Wright ordered his men forward, across the summit of the Dump to Fosse Alley.

Although it would have been wise to stop and seek out the troops in Fosse 8, Lieutenant-Colonel Wright adhered to his original orders. The Gordons moved off knowing little of the true situation to their left. One company of the 8th Black Watch and a number of Seaforths joined them, weakening Lord Lochiel's hold on the colliery. They advanced across open fields towards Haisnes, half a mile to the north east of Fosse 8. Pekin Trench, part of the German Second Line, covered the village and if any Germans held it the Gordons were doomed.

By 9.00am the 9th (Scottish) Division was in danger of breaking up. The leading battalions of 28 Brigade were finished, while the supports waited for further instructions. The Germans opposite this flank had so far held their ground and their machine guns were continuing to rake the buildings around Fosse 8. On the right, 26 Brigade was in a dilemma. Even though it had broken through and taken Hohenzollern Redoubt and Fosse 8, it had suffered severe casualties. Lord Lochiel had wisely decided to hold on until reserves arrived. Meanwhile, a single battalion, the 8th Gordons, was pushing on alone towards the German Second Line.

Sizeable reinforcements were needed to exploit 26 Brigade's success. If the reserve brigade could move forward quickly, Haisnes could be taken, destabilising the German positions west of Auchy-lès-Mines. There was still a chance that I Corps could achieve its objectives, but time was running out.

The Scots were completely exposed as they advanced towards the German Second Line. IWM Q28968

Chapter Six

7th DIVISION

22 Brigade's attack

Brigadier-General Julian Steele's 22 Brigade would attack on the left of 7th Division's front, with the 2nd Royal Warwickshires on the left and the 1st South Staffordshires on the right. The 1st Royal Welch Fusiliers would follow in support with the 2nd Queen's in Brigade reserve. Due to the proximity of Big Willie Trench, the 2nd Royal Warwickshires had been unable to complete their assembly trenches, forcing Lieutenant-Colonel Lefroy's men into an awkward re-entrant. On the right, the 1st South Staffordshires held a conventional system of assembly trenches well served with a network of communications trenches. Although the new assembly trenches (or battle trenches as they were known in 1915) had halved the width of No Man's Land, the assault troops still had to cross four hundred metres of open ground before they reached Quarry Trench.

Grass concealed the wire protecting the German trenches and the artillery had experienced great difficulty in registering hits on the entanglement. Spurn Head sap, opposite the centre of the Brigade front, had kept raiding parties at bay during the nights before the battle. Two strongpoints reinforced the German position. Pope's Nose Redoubt faced the centre of the Staffords' line and its machine-guns

7th Division dispositions at zero hour.

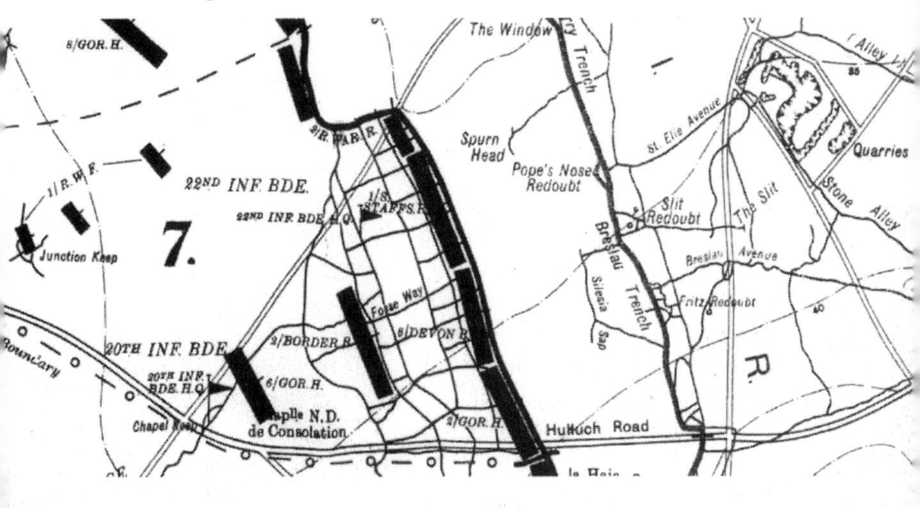

From their trenches the Germans had a perfect field of fire as the men cut through the wire. IWM - Q28978

could sweep the whole of the Brigade front. Slit Redoubt formed part of the support trench opposite 22 Brigade's right flank and it was capable of sheltering over one hundred men. The redoubt was an all round defensive position, capable of standing alone if the support trench was taken.

As zero hour approached everything seemed to be going to plan. The wind appeared to be carrying the gas forward and retaliation from the German artillery was light. As soon as the men began to climb the ladders and form up the German machine-guns opened fire, shooting blind into the smoke. Many were hit, and Lieutenant-Colonel Betrain Lefroy DSO and his adjutant, Captain Duke, were two of the first to fall. The Warwickshires situation deteriorated rapidly as they approached Quarry Trench. The smoke screen began to fade away short of the German wire, exposing the men to accurate fire. To their dismay, they could see that the entanglement had hardly been damaged by the bombardment and many of those equipped with wire-cutters were killed as they tried to cut a way through. With no way forward, the advance faltered.

The Staffordshires had a similar experience in front of Pope's Nose Redoubt. Heavy fire from the Slit struck the men as they emerged from the smoke. Yet again the entanglement proved to be inpenetrable. Three company commanders were shot down in front of the wire trying to rally their men forward, Captain Henry de Trafford and Lieutenant William Cooper were killed and Lieutenant Burke was wounded. Meanwhile, the 1st Royal Welch Fusiliers moved forward through the smoke in support, unaware of the deadlock ahead. It seemed as though 22 Brigade's attack was doomed to fail.

With grim determination the men crawled forward, clawing and clipping at the wire. Private Arthur Vickers led the way on the Royal Warwickshires front, cutting a way through in two places. Vickers survived and was rewarded with the Victoria Cross. Meanwhile, Captains Cartwright and O'Connor, two of the Welch Fusiliers senior officers, set to work reorganising the men ready to advance again. Before long gaps began to appear in the wire, allowing the advance to resume. The German gunners targeted the narrow openings and many were struck down as they threaded their way through. The majority of Germans fled down St Elie Avenue towards Hulluch Quarries when the first men entered the fire trench. Second Lieutenant Dibden led a party of bombers in pursuit, while the handful of remaining officers formed up the rest of the Brigade beyond the German support trench. It had taken over an hour to clear the German trench system, and the attack had cost 22 Brigade dearly. For once Brigade headquarters knew how the advance was progressing. The Brigade war diary reports how Lieutenant-Colonel R Ovens established the communications link:

Private Arthur Vickers VC.

When the men carrying the telephone were hit, he carried the wire forward himself into the German trenches and thus enabled touch to be kept with his Battalion.

Meanwhile, the Staffordshires had been unable to silence the two strongpoints on their front. As the Brigade advanced up the slope towards the Quarries they found themselves under fire from the rear. Fortunately, help was at hand. One of 20 Brigade's support battalions, the 2nd Borders, had managed to reach Gun Trench without encountering serious resistance. Having seen the Staffordshires in difficulty, Lieutenant-Colonel E Thorpe took the initiative, sending Captain Sutcliffe with the Battalion bombers to assist. Captain Ostle followed, leading two platoons of D Company back down the communications trenches. Sutcliffe's men attacked the Pope's Nose from the flank and rear and, after a stiff fight, seventy Germans

The open slope facing 22 Brigade: the Quarries are on the horizon while Cité St Elie remains hidden behind the crest. IWM - Q42185

surrendered. Soon afterwards the Staffordshires, aided by Ostle's men, silenced the Slit. One hundred and twenty prisoners and a number of machine-guns were taken, and escorted to the rear.

The 2nd Queen's were supposed to follow the rest of the Brigade through to the Quarries. The lead company, Captain Philpot's C Company, advanced east as expected, meeting the rest of the Brigade before the Quarries. Second Lieutenant Chapman entered the maze of mine workings with two platoons, taking forty prisoners in their dug-outs. However, the rest of the Battalion entered Quarry Trench north of where the Warwickshires had crossed, encountering stiff resistance. Lieutenant-Colonel Maurice Heath's men began to bomb their way along the German trenches even though they were urgently required to support the rest of the brigade. Lieutenant Taylor-Jones led the Queen's after Captain Brocklehurst fell wounded and his men eventually met the Scots at the end of Big Willie Trench.

Although Cité St Elie was within their sights, 22 Brigade no longer existed as a coherent fighting force. Even so, individual officers stuck to their orders, urging men forward in the hope of reinforcements. Lieutenant-Colonel Heath pushed on with the 2nd Queen's, entering Cité Trench west of the village. His men captured sixty prisoners and it appeared as though the village beyond was deserted. However, with less than three hundred men left of his command, Heath decided to wait in Cité Trench until reserves arrived. At the same time Lieutenant-Colonel Ovens led a party of the Staffords to the southern edge of the village, via Alley 1 communications trench. In the village Germans could be seen running to the rear. He could also see that a strong wire entanglement protected Puits Trench. In the meantime a mixed group of Staffords and Welch Fusiliers attempted to advance across the open towards the village. Although most of the Cité St Elie garrison had fled, the few that had stayed behind easily repulsed the weak attack. With the threat to their front eliminated the Germans turned their attentions on Ovens' party, forcing him to withdraw to the Quarries.

Brigadier-General Steele's Brigade was finished. Although his men had managed to clear the German front line trenches, they were unable to take the second line. Reinforcements were urgently needed so that Cité St Elie could be entered. It was going to be a race against time.

20 Brigade's attack

7th Division's right hand sector was held by 20 Brigade, led by Brigadier-General the Honourable John Trefusis. The Brigade held the sector north of the Vermelles - Hulluch road, where it would advance

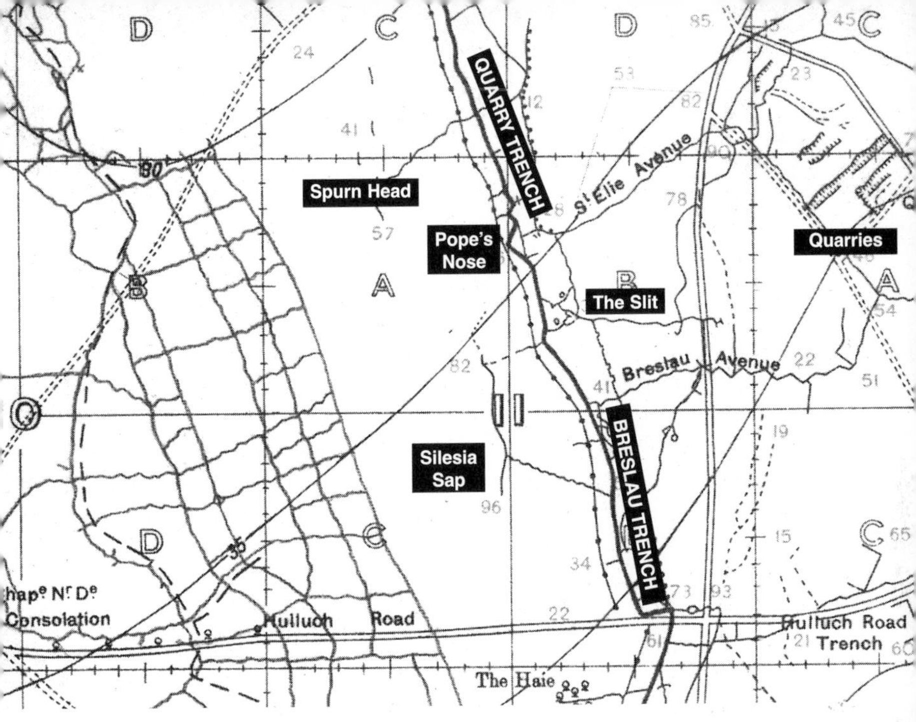

Trench map covering 7th Division's front.

alongside 1st Division, part of Sir Henry Rawlinson's IV Corps. The Brigade had undergone a major change in August. Two New Army battalions, the 8th and 9th Devonshires, replaced two Guards battalions when they left to join the Guards Division. The 8th Devonshires was to lead the left of the attack while the 2nd Gordon Highlanders advanced alongside the Hulluch Road. The 2nd Borders and 1/6th Gordon Highlanders would follow in support, while the 9th Devonshires remained in reserve.

For once there was ample space to deploy. The Brigade was adequately served by a series of new assembly trenches, which had halved the width of No Man's Land to four hundred metres. In many ways the sector was consistent with the sector to the north. A sap, known to the British as Silesia Sap, was used to observe the British as they dug their trenches; it also kept marauding night patrols away from the wire that protected Breslau Trench. Two redoubts reinforced the German trench system; Fritz Redoubt stood opposite the centre of 20 Brigade, while Hussey Redoubt blocked the Hulluch Road.

When the gas release began, many found that their gas helmets proved to be worthless, as illustrated in the 2nd Gordon's war diary:

The old smoke helmet is of little value, for if saved from the gas, one is compelled to breathe expired air.

British charge the German line with bombs and bayonets.

Weighed down by their heavy loads, the men struggled to breathe. Some fell victim to the poisonous fumes after ripping off their smoke helmets in desperation. Although the Germans could not see what was happening, they continued to fire wildly at the gas cloud. On the 8th Devonshires front, Lieutenant-Colonel Grant had planned to lead with C Company, with A and D following in support. However, the scheme began to go wrong at an early stage:

On the signal being given C, A and D Companies seemed to all go forward together in one line, this happened probably because A and D Companies started too soon .... Another result of the excessive speed with which the attack was started was that the front three Companies seem to have caught up 'Accessory No 1' and casualties occurred from the effects of this.

As the men emerged from the gas they were silhouetted against the white cloud, presenting the Germans with clear targets. To make matters worse, the artillery had only partially damaged the barbed wire:

The result was great crowding towards the gaps and consequent increase in casualties - most of which occurred just astride or in the midst of the wire in front of BRESLAU TRENCH.

Casualties were enormous; Lieutenant-Colonel Alexander Grant and Captain Arthur Kekewich lay dead, Major Carden and all but three of the remaining officers were wounded. Over seven hundred other ranks had become casualties. Captain Gwynn and Second Lieutenant Trott headed the small group of survivors storming Breslau Trench, only to find that most of the Germans had fled at the last moment. Considering that the men had never seen action before, it was a tremendous achievement.

There had been delays opening the cylinders on the 2nd Gordon Highlanders' front and at zero hour gas was still being pumped out into No Man's Land. Lieutenant-Colonel John Stansfield was anxious to avoid any delay and ordered his men forward through the swirling clouds. Although a large number collapsed gassed, the rest pushed on to the sounds of Piper Munro's bagpipes. The machine-gun in Hussey Redoubt traversed backwards and forwards, inflicting grievous casualties on the Highlanders. Meanwhile, the artillery battery in Gun Trench, beyond the crest, showered No Man's

Lt-Col Stansfield.

Land with shrapnel. Although the wire had been damaged, many were struck down as they threaded a way through the entanglement. The Battalion was virtually leaderless before it reached the German fire trench; Lieutenant-Colonel Stansfield DSO had been mortally wounded, Captain James Boyd had been killed and Captain MacTavish lay wounded. Even so, the Gordons pushed on through the broken wire and into Breslau Trench. The Battalion bombers overwhelmed Hussey Redoubt, while the rest of the men pressed on to the support line taking fifty prisoners.

The Devonshires and the Gordon Highlanders pressed on towards Gun Trench, still under fire from the gun battery. At the summit of the hill a brisk fight took place with small groups of Germans who had fled at the start of the attack. They were quickly overcome and the two battalions carried on down the reverse slope. Through the clouds of smoke emerged the shapes of four guns, their muzzles smoking. Sergeant Northam led a charge and although the gun crews scattered, many were captured soon afterwards. Pausing momentarily the two battalions each claimed two guns; proudly chalked their names on their trophies. The heaps of empty shell cases in the gun pits showed that the guns had been firing all morning.

The depleted battalions pushed on towards the German Second Line, advancing in a single line with their right flank on the Hulluch road. At 8.30am Captain Thomas Finlay and about one hundred Gordons reached Estaminet Corner on the Lens - La Bassée Road. As

Captured guns on display in Bethune. IWM - Q28964

Looking east towards Hulluch from Estaminet Corner. IWM - Q41996

they began to dig in, they watched as a column of infantry entered Cité St Elie from the east. It was the reserve battalion of the 11th Reserve Regiment. It had been roused from its billets in Wingles when the attack began. As soon as the column turned into the main street Finlay ordered his men to open fire scattering the Germans. Seeking cover in the houses that lined the street, they began to man the defences around Cité St Elie.

The men at the front now wondered where the rest of the Brigade was. Part of the 2nd Borders had gone back to help the Staffordshires clear the strongpoints on 22 Brigade's front. Lieutenant-Colonel

German trenches guarding Cité St Elie; the second line skirts the western edge of the village. The gun pits can be seen either side of the Hulluch road.

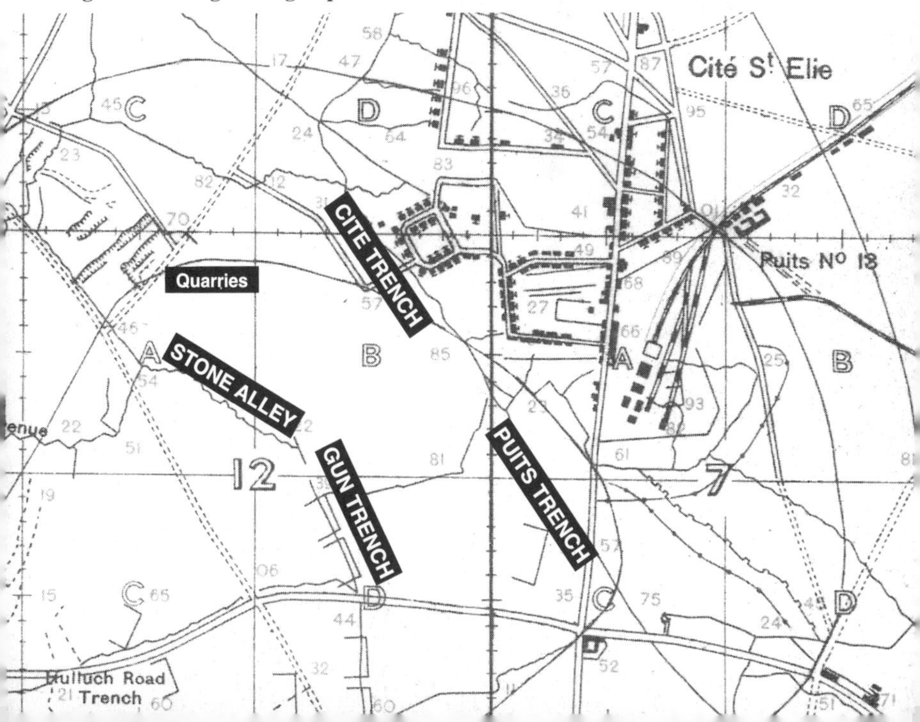

Thorpe was reluctant to move forward before 22 Brigade caught up on his left. He waited on the line of Gun Trench, with the 1/6th Gordons alongside. Meanwhile, the 9th Devonshires had been shot to pieces before they had reached Gun Trench. The Germans, scattered by Finlay's Highlanders, had managed to occupy Puits Trench, and they were now positioned to stop the Brigade moving forward.

About 10.00am two companies of the 1/6th Gordons joined their sister battalion at the crossroads, suffering heavy casualties as they moved forward. Believing that the rest of the Brigade would be following, Major Ross prepared to reconnoitre the German positions to his front. Captain Finlay led a party of fifty men forward and they almost reached the German wire before they were seen. Finlay was killed and the few that made it back reported a strong German presence. Second Lieutenant Ian McPherson tried a different approach, taking fifteen bombers forward along a communications trench. They too were discovered and McPherson died, along with most of his party. Major Ross had enough information to convince him that strong reinforcements were needed before an advance could be attempted. Having sent an urgent appeal to Brigade to that effect, Ross set his men to work digging a defensive position.

Chapter Seven

THE BATTLE CONTINUES

27 Brigade advance towards Haisnes

9th Division's scheme expected its reserve brigade, under Brigadier-General Clarence Bruce, to follow the two leading brigades as far as Haisnes village. Once the German Second Line fell into Scottish hands, 27 Brigade would take over the advance towards the Haute Deule Canal. However, the plan had broken down at an early stage; 28 Brigade was still in its own trenches and 26 Brigade was holding Fosse 8, but in no condition to advance any further. There was, however, a glimmer of hope on the right flank, where the 8th Gordon Highlanders had gone ahead alone towards Haisnes.

27 Brigade began moving forward from their trenches, between Cambrin and Vermelles, shortly after zero hour. Brigadier-General Bruce had two sets of orders. The first assumed that 26 Brigade had captured Hohenzollen Redoubt or Fosse 8, in which case Bruce's

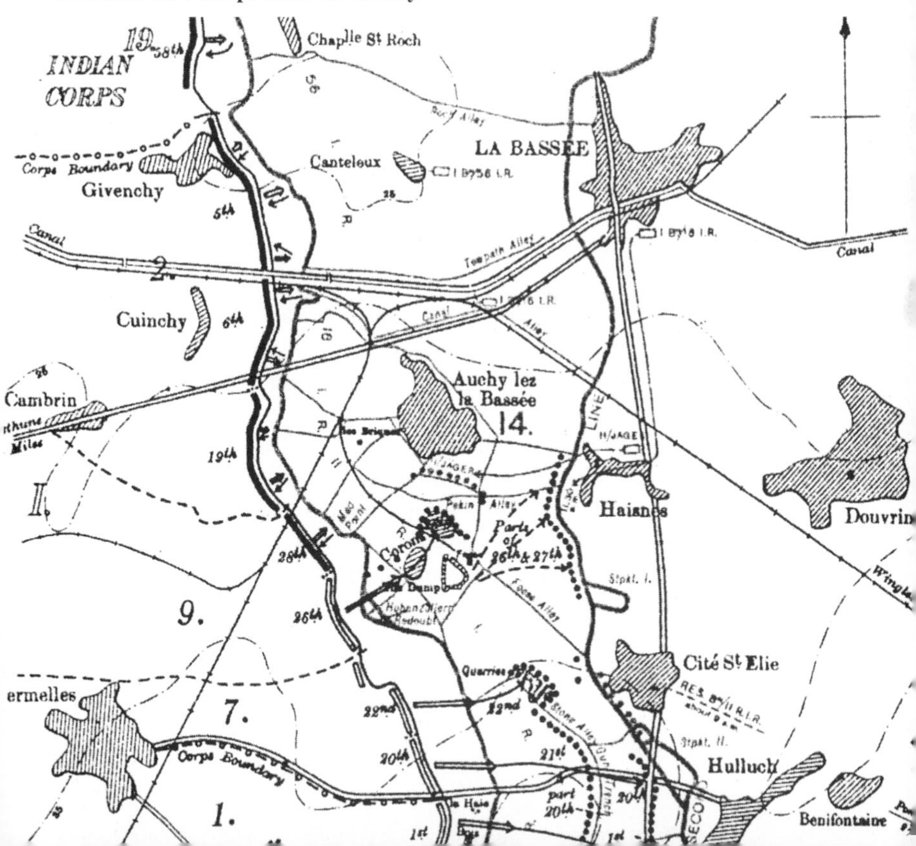

Situation on I Corps front at midday.

Brigade would push on towards Haisnes. The alternative plan presumed that 26 Brigade had failed in its task and 27 Brigade would then have to renew the attack.

At 8.00am Brigadier-General Bruce received notification that Fosse 8 had been secured, and immediately ordered his three leading battalions to advance. Unfortunately, the Brigade was struggling to make any headway against the tide of wounded and only the 12th Royal Scots were in a position to carry out the order. Lieutenant-Colonel G Loch led his men past the Dump, taking Douvrin church tower as his bearing. He reached Pekin Trench at 8.45am, finding the 8th Gordons in the process of consolidating the trench. Without delay Lieutenant-Colonel Loch ordered his men forward:

> *The Battalion then advanced through the 8th Gordons in one line. Advance was carried out by rushes for 300 yards. We were then unable to advance further, being entirely unsupported and subjected to heavy enfilade fire from HAISNES and CITE St ELIE on both flanks, as well as from the front.*

The moment had passed; with both villages in German hands, the chances of breaking through to open country were diminishing rapidly.

The second of Brigadier-General Bruce's battalions, the 11th Royal Scots, was supposed to follow behind 28 Brigade. It had, however, been unable to move very far. Ignorant of the disaster that had befallen 28 Brigade, Lieutenant-Colonel R C Dundas led his Battalion into already congested trenches. Hundreds of wounded men making their way back to the dressing stations blocked the way, and for two hours the 11th Royal Scots hardly moved. With time passing, Dundas decided to make a detour around the area in the hope that they could rejoin the rest of the Brigade:

> *It was found that the 12th Royal Scots would have advanced by this time and, as the 11th were to move in their support, the commanding officer decided to abandon the original plan of moving up the saps in rear of 28th I.B. and instead to proceed along the Reserve Trench and down a forward Communications trench.*

The Battalion eventually left the British trenches at 9.30am, an hour later than planned. Having skirted the east side of the Dump, the Battalion inexplicably became separated into two. The officer leading the first two companies mistook Haisnes church as the direction for advance and came under fire from machine-guns in Auchy Cemetery to their left. Realising their mistake the half Battalion wheeled to their right and moved east towards Haisnes. They found a thick belt of wire

The open ground north east of the Dump, the outskirts of Haisnes can be seen on the horizon. IWM - Q42189

protecting Pekin Trench and began to cut a way through, hoping to enter the unoccupied trench. It was too late. The reserve battalion of the German 16th Regiment had already reached Haisnes. They set up their machine-guns, scattering the Royal Scots as they floundered on the wire. The rest of Battalion reached Pekin Trench relatively unscathed, and by 11.45am they were established alongside their sister battalion.

The 10th Argyll & Sutherland Highlanders eventually reached Fosse Alley at midday, six hours after it set off. Hearing that the position in front of Douvrin was strongly held, Lieutenant-Colonel Mackenzie decided to wait for further instructions. From now on the Scots would be on the defensive. With the Germans holding Haisnes and Cité St Elie there was no way forward. The men in Pekin Trench found themselves isolated and under attack; the 12th Royal Scots war

Area east of Fosse 8, the German Second Line is under construction in front of Haisnes.

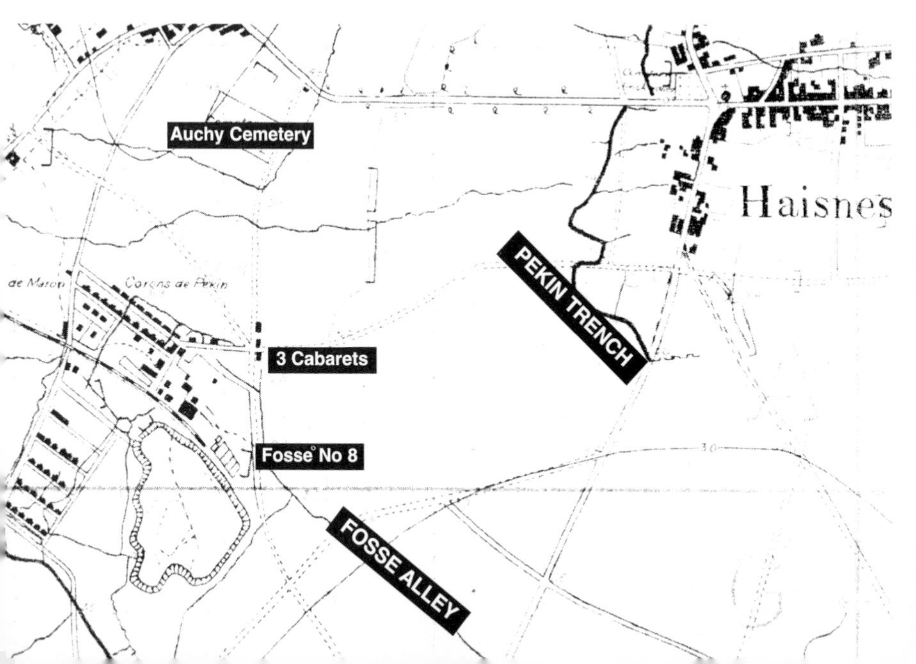

diary sums up the situation:

.... Our right was in the air and being enfiladed from CITÉ ST ELIE; our left was also enfiladed from HAISNES and being attacked by bombers down PEKIN TRENCH.

At 1.30pm the Argylls sent a single company forward in response to a call for reinforcements. Hardly any made it across to Pekin Trench alive, and it would only be a matter of time before the Royal Scots broke. While artillery batteries north and east of Haisnes pounded the position, bombing parties began closing in.

28 Brigade renews the attack

Although over half its strength had been engaged, 28 Brigade had failed to enter the German trenches west of Fosse 8. Brigade-General ScraseDickins knew little of the situation on his own front, but Major-General Thesiger was adamant that his men tried again. If 28 Brigade could enter the German trenches, the colliery could be secured. The 9th Scottish Rifles faced Madagascar Trench and Lieutenant-Colonel Northey had so far managed to convince his superiors that another attack would be pointless. Meanwhile, the 11th Highland Light Infantry had already sent two of its companies towards Little Willie Trench.

The Brigade was finally ordered to attack at noon, but the decision was taken too late to inform the two battalions. As zero hour approached Lieutenant-Colonel Northey received a series of bewildering messages and the frustration is evident in his report:

At 11.53am I received the order for the Brigade to attack at 12 noon. I have since heard that a message was sent out from the Brigade timed 11.57am prolonging the bombardment till 12.15pm and consequently the attack. I did not receive this message..........In view of my order to attack 'sharp' at 12 noon, and only knowing then that I could count on heavy covering fire up to that hour, I moved my first line over the parapet at 12.05pm closely followed by my second line.

The two companies were immediately struck by machine-gun fire from Railway redoubt and rifle fire from Madagascar Trench. Northey promptly called off the attack and the survivors withdrew under covering fire from the Battalion machine guns. Meanwhile, the Highland Light Infantry received the order to advance at 12.03pm, three minutes late. 'D' Company and half of 'C' Company were immediately stood to, however, a few minutes later a second message arrived, postponing the attack until 12.15pm. As ordered the six

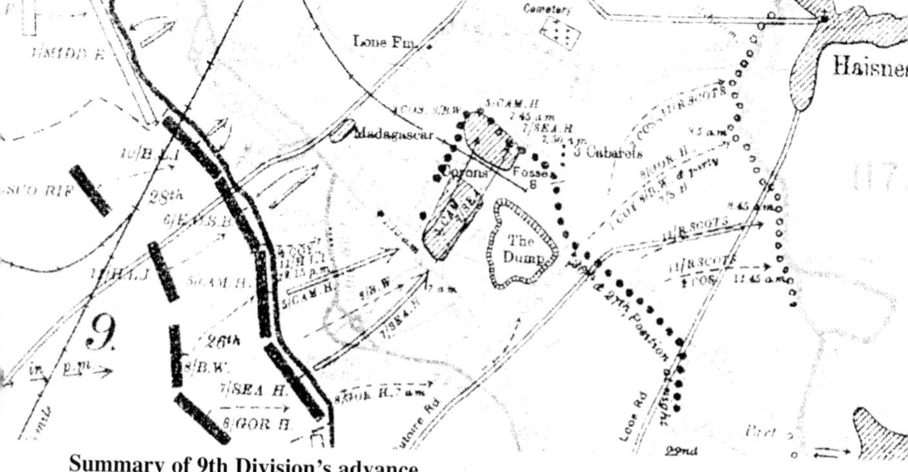

Summary of 9th Division's advance.

platoons climbed into the open, where they were met by crossfire from Mad Point and Strongpoint. They stood no chance of advancing and Lieutenant-Colonel Fergusson could do no more than recall the survivors. The two battalions had lost heavily, a combined total of over four hundred casualties. 28 Brigade was finished and there would be no more attacks on Madagacar Trench.

Meanwhile, the men holding Fosse 8 waited in vain for reinforcements. Throughout the afternoon 26 Brigade sheltered from the German shells as best they could, anxiously awaiting assistance. The only consolation was that the Germans were powerless to counter-attack, they too needed reinforcements.

21 Brigade advances on Cité St Elie

By midday all forward movement had stopped on 7th Division's front. Part of the 2nd Queen's was in Puits Trench to the west of Cité St Elie in touch with the Scots. Lieutenant-Colonel Ovens was consolidating a defensive line around Hulluch Quarries with the rest of 22 Brigade. On the right a thin line of troops belonging to 20 Brigade faced Hulluch, while the rest of the Brigade remained pinned down in Gun Trench. Both brigades had lost heavily and fresh reinforcements were now needed to exploit the breakthrough. In the meantime German reserves had started to arrive. At 9.30am the reserve battalion of the 11th Reserve Infantry Regiment had entered Cité St Elie. A second battalion, of the 157th Regiment, reached Hulluch around midday.

Brigadier-General Herbert Watts' 21 Brigade eventually managed to reach the old assembly trenches after a six hour journey. The flood of wounded men blocking the communication trenches had forced the Brigade into the open. So far Major-General Capper believed that 22 Brigade was held up in No Man's Land. Based on this erroneous

21 Brigade had to deploy on the reverse slope of the Grenay Ridge before advancing on Puits Trench, Cité St Elie Mine can be seen on the horizon.

information, Watts was instructed to exploit the gap made by 20 Brigade and head towards Hulluch. As the Brigade prepared to cross No Man's Land Brigadier Watts received new orders. Major-General Capper, now aware that 22 Brigade was making its way towards Cité St Elie, wanted 21 Brigade split in half.

At 11.30am the 2nd Green Howards headed towards Puits Trench, with the 1/4th Cameron Highlanders in support. As soon as they passed the Quarries, the Germans in Cité St Elie opened fire, causing heavy casualties. Facing a hopeless task, the Green Howards stopped, occupying Stone Alley. The Camerons joined them shortly afterwards, extending their line as far north as the Quarries.

The rest of the Brigade advanced north of the Hulluch road. The 2nd Wiltshires and the 2nd Bedfordshires came under fire from Puits Trench as soon as they crossed the summit of the Grenay Ridge. Seeing the uncut wire in front of *Stutzpunkt* II, the advance faltered at Gun Trench. Over five hundred had fallen and it seemed unwise to continue. Two platoons of the Bedfords attempted to advance further, but few returned alive. 21 Brigade had been brought to a standstill and 7th Division had no more reserves.

At 2.00pm the Queen's noticed that the Gemans were beginning to evacuate Cité St Elie. Lieutenant-Colonel Maurice Heath and Captain Philpot led their men into the village in pursuit and for a short time it seemed as though the breakthrough had come. Their chance to exploit the opportunity was, however, cut short by artillery fire, most of it from British guns. With his group in danger of being cut off, Heath withdrew his men and the majority retired to the safety of the Quarries. A few stayed on in Cité Trench under Lieutenant-Colonel Heath and they eventually withdrew alongside the Scots under cover of darkness.

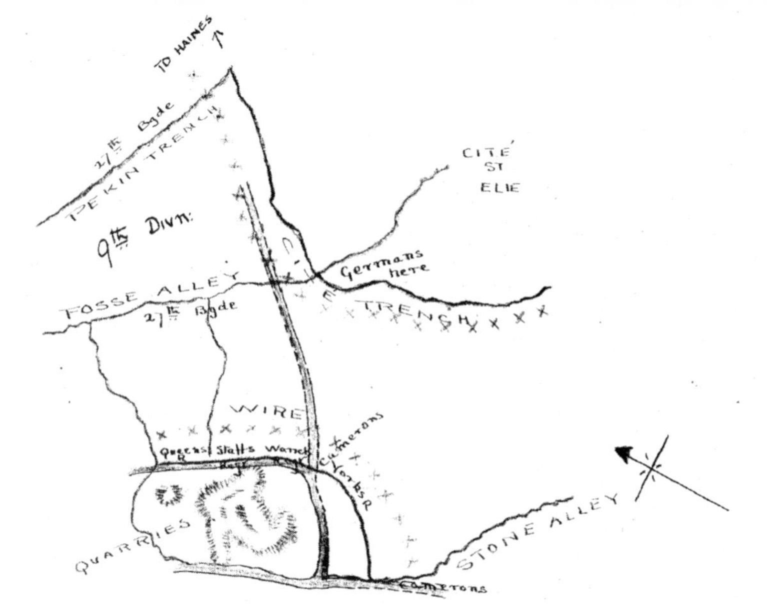

22 Brigade's defence of the Hulluch Quarries during the afternoon.

Meanwhile, Lieutenant-Colonel Ovens sent two officer patrols out along the communications trenches from the Quarries. Having studied the defence line in front of Cité St Elie they concluded that:

> *The enemy's second line strongly held on northern and western edges of the village with rifles and machine-guns; houses loop-holed and a strong wire obstacle in front of Cité Trench undamaged by our bombardment.*

Major-General Capper was anxious to take the village before dark and ordered his artillery to shell the village in preparation for an attack at 4.00pm. The Wiltshires and the Bedfords watched as the shells fell on the houses, missing the real threat, Puits Trench. Although the

Summary of 7th Division's advance.

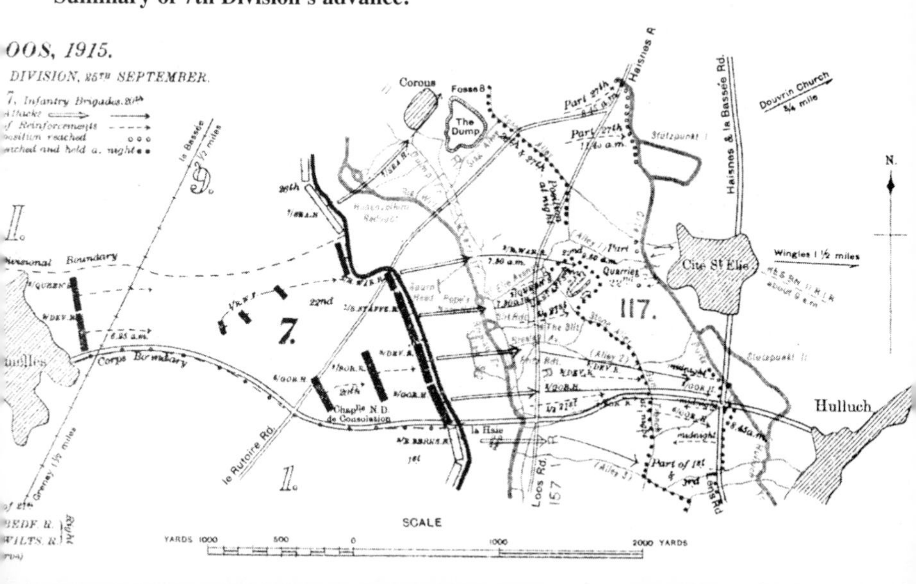

bombardment looked impressive to the artillery observers, those at the front could see that it had failed to do little more than raise clouds of dust. Lieutenant-Colonel Leatham, the Wiltshires CO, appealed against the attack. Major-General Capper relented and the assault was called off. For the time being the men would consolidate a position on the line of Stone Alley and Gun Trench. Plans were being formulated for a morning assault and Capper wanted to preserve his scant reserve.

DUSK UNTIL DAWN

As daylight began to fade on the 25th the men of I Corps faced an uneasy night. 2nd Division had not moved since the morning. It had, however, mustered a scratch brigade of three battalions (not committed in the morning assault), under Lieutenant-Colonel Carter, to aid 9th and 7th Divisions. 9th Division held an awkward salient around Fosse 8. 28 Brigade was still in its original trenches facing Mad Point, while most of what was left of 26 Brigade (about 500 men) held a thin perimeter around the buildings of the colliery. One battalion of 27 Brigade held Fosse Alley, north of the Dump, in touch with 7th Division's troops. However, most of 27 Brigade was in Pekin Trench, in danger of being cut off. 7th Division had recalled its advanced parties from Cité St Elie and 22 Brigade held a perimeter around Hulluch Quarries. 20 Brigade held outposts on the Lens - La Bassée road in touch with IV Corps, while 21 Brigade dug in along Stone Alley and Gun Trench.

27 Brigade withdraw from Pekin Trench

As the light faded 27 Brigade's position in Pekin Trench was becoming perilous. Although Brigadier-General Bruce had sent two companies of the 6th Royal Scots Fusiliers to support the position late in the afternoon, it was a case of too little too late. The Royal Scots war diary sums up the predicament they faced:

> *Darkness was setting in and the situation was critical. Our bombs, being soaked with rain, were useless, and the men's rifles were clogged with mud. The flanks, particularly the left, became very unsteady, and it was necessary to rally the men three times and to reoccupy PEKIN TRENCH, which the men had been leaving in large numbers.*

Unable to contact their Brigadier, the senior officers conferred and decided to abandon Pekin Trench before they were overrun. With great difficulty the Scots managed to extricate themselves without raising the Germans suspicions. As they fell back towards Fosse Alley, the 10th Argylls thought for a moment that they were under attack:

A great mass of troops appeared on our front about 1000 yards away. At first we thought they were the enemy, but they turned out to be our own troops retiring. The confusion was great and the mixture of units also. Every attempt was made by the officers of this battalion to rally the fugitives, unfortunately with but little success, and they passed right through us leaving the Battalion with its flanks exposed.

It took all night to reorganise battalions into a defensive line along Fosse Alley. Fortunately, the Germans were also in a state of disarray, and they too spent the night consolidating their positions.

73 Brigade takes over Fosse 8

During the morning of the 25th, General Haig allocated a single brigade from the reserve, the 73rd, to I Corps front. The rest of his reserve was be used to exploit a gap created on IV Corps front. Brigadier-General William Oswald's men had not experienced trench warfare, never mind a full-scale battle; all they possessed was enthusiasm. 24th Division had only landed in France four weeks earlier, and after a brief period of acclimatisation had been ordered to move to the Bethune area. With little time to spare, the troops carried out three night marches, covering over fifty miles in total.

By noon on the 25th it was obvious that 9th Division had suffered grievous casualties and would struggle to maintain its hold on Fosse 8 and the Dump. At 1.00pm General Gough ordered 73 Brigade forward from its billets at Beuvry, with orders to secure the colliery. He instructed Brigadier Oswald to:

Form a defensive flank on the line - junction of Slag and Fosse Alleys - Three Cabarets - Corons de Pekin - Corons de Maron - Mad Point back to our own trenches. Actual line is to be selected by Brigadier.

It interesting to note that the orders indicate that I Corps believed that Mad Point had been captured, even at this late stage. With such limited and vague instructions it is obvious that Lieutenant-General Gough knew little of the true situation on 9th Division's front.

Although the men of 73 Brigade were eager to get to grips with the enemy, many were concerned about the lack of experience the men had. The war diary of the 9th Royal Sussex sums up the situation:

It is regretted that before being launched into such a

In the dark, the battlefield was a bewildering experience for 73 Brigade.
IWM Q28966

> *desperate action steps had not been taken to accustom the men to war conditions.*

The Brigade was poorly equipped to undertake a defensive action, each battalion only had two heavy Maxim guns; nobody had seen or used the new, lighter Lewis guns. It is also doubtful if the Brigade carried a supply of bombs up to the front line. Without them, they were virtually defenceless in close-quarter fighting. Again it is unsure if the men had used or even seen a bomb.

As the men marched towards the rumble of battle, they had to force their way through a tide of wounded and ambulances. They made slow progress, and it was dark before the Brigade reached the old front line. Without guides the men became disorientated in the trenches and confused by the constant stopping and starting. Two companies of the 12th Royal Fusiliers lost their way, and in an effort to relocate them, Major H W Compton led the rest of his Battalion out of the trenches. When the moon emerged from behind a cloud they were spotted and came under heavy shellfire. Compton's party took cover and were eventually found by the Brigade Major of 22 Brigade. They spent the next three days, with the 7th Division, near Hulluch Quarries.

The rest of the Brigade took all night to find and relieve the Scots. As shells fell amongst them, Oswald's men tried to form a defensive line around the burning buildings. Dawn found the 7th Northamptons holding the west and north faces of Fosse 8, supported by a mixed group of Scottish stragglers. The remaining two companies of the 12th Royal Fusiliers held the centre of the line, a right angle salient centred on Three Cabarets road junction. On the right of the Brigade, the 9th Royal Sussex held Fosse Alley with the Dump to their rear. For the time being it looked as though the colliery was secure; the question was for how long.

Counterattacks on 7th Division

After discussions at divisional and corps level it had been agreed that 7th Division would reorganise its front over night. Cité St Elie was strongly defended by Puits Trench and it would be unwise to conduct a frontal attack on the village. Instead the Division would push east past Hulluch, in conjunction with 1st Division. This meant that the front needed to be reorganised before dawn. The Cameron Highlanders and the Green Howards were ordered to withdraw from the Quarries, leaving 22 Brigade to cover their sector. They moved south to the Hulluch road and were joined by the 2nd Royal Scots Fusiliers, 7th Division's last reserve. Meanwhile, Carter's force, the three battalions from 2nd Division, mustered alongside.

With great difficulty the reorganisation was completed by 11.00pm. Unfortunately, in the darkness the sector vacated by the Cameron Highlanders was left partially unoccupied. Although the British troops failed to notice the blunder, the Germans seized on the opportunity. What happened next will probably always remain a mystery. At 11.20pm Brigadier-General Steele was notified that the Germans had infiltrated the Quarries. A company of the Green Howards was immediately ordered back into the Quarries to drive them out. However, before the Green Howards arrived, a second party of Germans had infiltrated the northern corner of the Quarries. Lieutenant-Colonel Heath and Captain Philpot of the 2nd Queen's valiantly tried to reorganise a counterattack to drive the Germans out. Captain Philpot's report is probably the only surviving account of what happened:

> *Shortly after 11pm somebody looked into the dug-out and stated 'that all the troops in front of us had retired at the double, and that our troops were being bombed out of their trench by*

A labyrinth of mine workings, presumed to be Hulluch Quarries.

View from Gun Trench across 20 Brigade's sector. IWM - Q41994

> *Germans following up.' The Germans bombed the Queen's from both flanks in the trench.*
>
> *Some dozen of us, comprising a General, the commanding officer, the adjutant, four company officers and myself, together with the regimental sergeant-major formed up in the Quarry. The first German we saw was promptly shot and we then dispersed a party on our right flank, about forty yards away. A party on our left flank was similarly fired on and scattered, when turning about we saw the enemy behind us. These we drove back with rifle and revolver fire, and after engaging the other parties of the enemy, it was decided to make a dash for it. When I left the Quarry, the Germans were about fifteen yards away, and I saw two men fall in front of me as killed. I think they must have been the General and the commanding officer as they are the only two now missing.*

The general was Brigadier-General Clarence Bruce, 27 Brigade's commanding officer. He had been in the process of reporting his overnight position, using 22 Brigade's telephone. Bruce survived the war in captivity. Lieutenant-Colonel Maurice Heath was killed as he tried to escape the Quarries.

About this time, Lieutenant-Colonels Ovens and Young of the 1st South Staffordshires and the 2nd Green Howards were on their way to meet General Bruce. Finding a German sentry guarding the signals dug-out, the two officers crept back to their men to organise a withdrawal. By providing covering fire for the rest of the Brigade, the two battalions ensured that the Germans did not exploit their success. A counter-attack by the 2nd Queen's failed to make headway in the darkness, and at daybreak 22 Brigade was holding a tentative foothold in the old German front line system.

While the fighting in the Quarries was underway, the right sector of the 7th Division also came under attack where 20 Brigade was holding Gun Trench and an advanced line north west of Hulluch. Around midnight elements of the 15th Reserve Regiment were among the wiring parties and sentries before the alarm was sounded. In the darkness the Gordon Highlanders and the Devonshires found themselves attacked both in the flanks and from rear:

> *The attack was pressed home in the endeavour to recapture the field guns in GUN TRENCH. The men in the forward positions gave way and fell back on GUN TRENCH and some even went back further than this, but were rallied by officers of the battalion and the Brigade-Major and taken back to help the men in GUN TRENCH. The enemy's foremost attackers actually reached GUN TRENCH and were killed almost on the parapet, whilst a good many others, estimated at anything between fifty and one hundred men, were killed in this attack which was beaten off.*

Although the outposts had been lost, 20 Brigade established a new forward line in Gun Trench under Brigadier-General Watts' supervision.

By now neither 7th Division nor I Corps had fresh reserves to retake the Quarries. All First Army could do was redirect a single New Army battalion, the 9th Norfolks, from IV Corps area south of the Hulluch road. It was intended that they would retake the Quarries at first light.

Although the Norfolks were at full strength, they were by no means fresh. Having endured a long night of marching and counter-marching across the dark battlefield, the men were exhausted. They were inexperienced too; the Battalion had only been in France for a few weeks and hardly a man had heard a shot fired in anger. At 6.45 am they advanced towards the Quarries by platoon rushes, as they had been taught in training. They formed perfect targets on the open battlefield and drew fire from every gun in range. Against an entrenched enemy they stood no chance; over four hundred were killed or wounded.

The attack brought an end to the fighting on the Quarries front for a time. Although the shelling and bombing attacks never relented, the sector stabilised. For the next two weeks I Corps would focus its attention on Fosse 8 and Hohenzollern Redoubt.

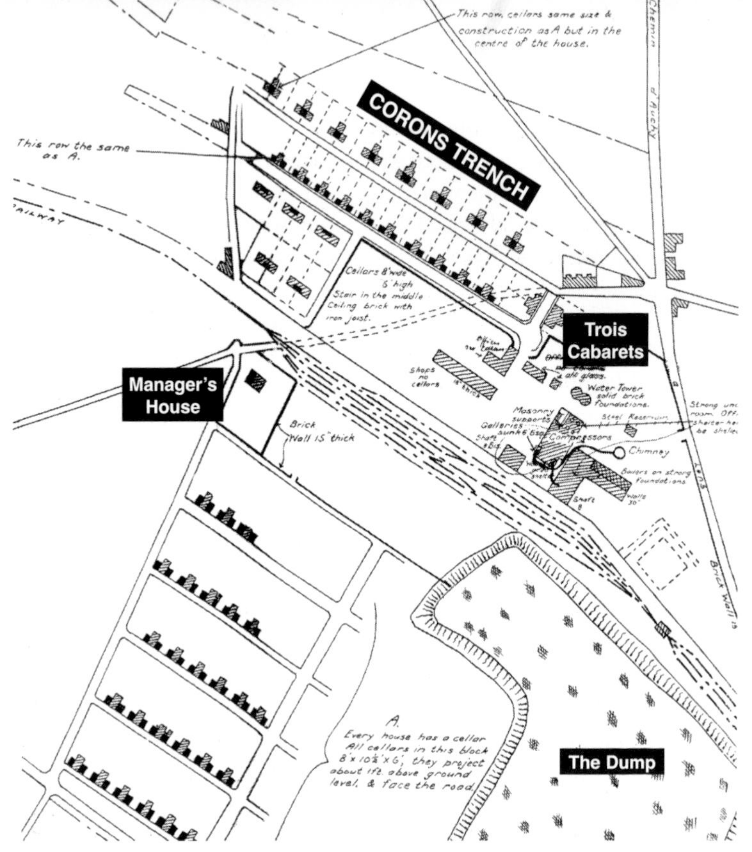

Detailed map of Fosse 8 and the Dump.

73 BRIGADE HOLDS FOSSE 8

The Germans made no attempt to attack Fosse 8 on the 26th, preferring to shell the colliery with shrapnel and high explosive. It was an unfortunate position, for the mine buildings served as excellent ranging targets. Although they were woefully inexperienced in all areas, 73 Brigade did what they could to improve their position. As the day wore on the incessant shelling began to take its toll on the men, and some showed signs of wavering. The fact that the supply system had broken down did little to bolster their morale, as the 13th Middlesex war diary illustrates:

> *....owing to the isolated position of the men in the front trenches, it was impossible to pass up supplies, except by night. On the Sunday and Monday nights a small quantity of water, biscuit and ammunition was sent from the companies in support trenches to those in front, but these men would have suffered*

much more severely if it had not been for the kindness of the 2nd Queen's Regiment who generously shared with them what rations they had.

Faced with such difficulties, Brigadier-General Oswald cracked under the pressure and he was replaced by Brigadier-General Rudolph Jelf. Jelf's report describes what he found:

No communication of any kind had been established with my battalions either by wire or orderly, and I attribute this to the fact that all battalions and the brigade staff were quite ignorant of the rudiments of what to do in the trenches; how communications were established, the method of drawing rations, etc., they never having been in trenches in their lives before. And I can confidently assert, after many months of trench warfare, that it would have taxed to the uttermost the resources of any Regular battalions, with plenty of experience behind them, to have kept themselves supplied, under similar circumstances.

Exhausted, hungry and thirsty, the men of 73 Brigade spent a second uneasy night holding the Fosse 8 perimeter.

Meanwhile, the Germans had been busy preparing to attack, and now that reinforcements had arrived they planned to recapture Fosse 8 and the Dump. Under the cover of darkness parties from the Composite Bavarian Regiment and 91st Reserve Regiment crept forward from Haisnes. At 5.00am, as dawn began to break, two red rockets signalled the start of the attack. Having very few machine-guns, for most had been destroyed or damaged, Jelf's men were powerless to stop their assailants. One party broke into the Northants position and proceeded to drive them from Corons Trench. Without bombs to reply, the Northants retired, taking cover amongst the mine buildings. A second lodgement was made at Three Cabarets in the centre of the brigade line. The Royal Sussex war diary describes the ensuing chaos;

.... They opened enfilade fire down the trenches occupied by A and B companies. The position of A company then became untenable and they were obliged to retire to the original support trench of the Germans.

The most serious blow fell on the right of the Royal Sussex, at the junction of Fosse Alley and Slag Alley. Bombing parties fanned out from the point of breakthrough, moving onto the summit of the Dump supported by machine gun teams. Finding themselves fired on from the rear, 73 Brigade began to retreat through the Corons.

Scattered parties tried in vain to keep the Germans at bay, but without bombs and with little ammunition left, it was only a matter of time before they were overwhelmed. Fortunately, the CO of the 8th Black Watch had prepared for such an eventuality:

At 8.30am Col. Cameron of Lochiel issued orders that a party of 70 men 8th Black Watch and 30 men 5th Cameron Highlanders under a captain were to go out to HOHENZOLLERN REDOUBT to rally any men of 73 Brigade who should retire from Fosse 8. Capt the Hon. F Bowes-Lyon and Lt C G C MacIntosh were sent out with this party, also a strong party of bombers.

The open ground beyond the redoubt was swept with bullets and Bowes-Lyon opted to hold the Trench known as East Face.

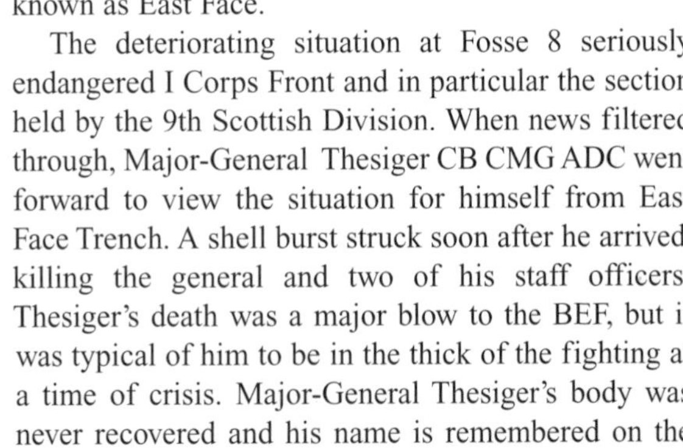

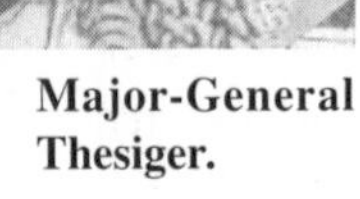

Major-General Thesiger.

The deteriorating situation at Fosse 8 seriously endangered I Corps Front and in particular the section held by the 9th Scottish Division. When news filtered through, Major-General Thesiger CB CMG ADC went forward to view the situation for himself from East Face Trench. A shell burst struck soon after he arrived, killing the general and two of his staff officers. Thesiger's death was a major blow to the BEF, but it was typical of him to be in the thick of the fighting at a time of crisis. Major-General Thesiger's body was never recovered and his name is remembered on the Loos Memorial at Dud Corner.

Around noon a determined German attack drove Jelf's command out of Fosse 8 and across the open ground towards Hohenzollern Redoubt. They found the Scots waiting for them in the East Face of the redoubt and many rallied to fire on the advancing Germans. Captain Fergus Bowes-Lyon (the Queen Mother's older brother) was killed and Lieutenant Charles McIntosh mortally wounded as they organised 73 Brigade into a coherent line. Bowes-Lyon's body was never found and his name is on the Loos Memorial to the Missing. McIntosh died at Chouques Casualty Clearing Station the following day, and was buried in the adjacent Military Cemetery.

While the assault on Fosse 8 was continuing, a German bombing party began working their way along Little Willie Trench in the hope of outflanking the Scots on the redoubt. The 8th Black Watch war diary outlines what steps were taken to drive them out:

Later in the morning orders were received for a Brigade Bombing party to go out to the redoubt and endeavour to bomb

Corporal James Pollock VC.

down LITTLE WILLIE where German bombers were much in evidence. A similar bombing party to be sent from 28 Brigade on the left to bomb down LITTLE WILLIE from that direction; no signs of the latter party were ever seen by us. Our party failed to make much headway as apparently German bombers could throw further and were using more powerful bombs.

The Germans would have been even more successful if it had not been for the bravery of Corporal James Pollock of the 5th Camerons. When it seemed as though the Scots were about to lose the struggle, Pollock scrambled out into the open with a satchel loaded with bombs. By hurling grenades down into the trench, he single handedly checked the Germans. For nearly an hour Pollock remained out in the open, thwarting all attempts to enter the redoubt. In recognition of his act of bravery Pollock was awarded the Victoria Cross. He was later commissioned to the 6th Battalion, but was eventually invalided out of the army following an accident with a rifle grenade.

General Haig was at Lieutenant-General Gough's headquarters when he heard of Thesiger's death. He immediately instructed Major-General Edward S Bulfin, whose 28th Division was approaching First Army area, to take over command of 9th Division's area of operations. Soon after Bulfin arrived at his new temporary command, orders arrived instructing a counterattack to take both Fosse and Dump

Scots on roll call after the battle.

Trenches. With his own troops deployed on route, Bulfin was to attack with what was left of 26 Brigade, numbering around six hundred men by this stage. Despite the ordeals of the past two days Brigadier-General Ritchie's troops advanced as asked. In the face of machine-gun and shellfire they were unable to progress any further than the eastern edge of Hohenzollen Redoubt. Their courage had, however, stiffen the resolve of the 73 Brigade, and for the time being Hohenzollen Redoubt remained in British hands. The fight for Fosse 8 and the redoubt had cost 26 Brigade dearly, over 2,100 Highlanders had been killed or wounded in less than seventy-two hours.

Chapter Eight

28th DIVISION OCCUPIES THE REDOUBT

Situation on I Corps front

As 26 September came to a close, it was obvious to First Army headquarters that the reserves initially allocated to its offensive had been insufficient. Two of XI Corps divisions had already been squandered in a futile attempt to bludgeon a way through south of Hulluch, on IV Corp front. The remaining infantry division of the reserve, the Guards, was due to attack the following day, again on IV Corps front east of Loos. Meanwhile, Lieutenant-General Hubert Gough, who had so far only received five battalions from the reserve, was in desperate need of support. All three of his divisions had suffered heavily on the opening day, and all his reserves had been committed. Although the front astride the La Bassée canal had settled down, elsewhere Gough's men were on the defensive. Having retaken the Quarries and Fosse 8, the Germans seemed determined to recover Hohenzollern Redoubt.

Field Marshal Sir John French had precious little reserves to spare, and the French Army was fully committed south of Lens and in the Champagne region. Major-General Edward Bulfin's 28th Division had only just arrived at Bailleul, expecting to rest after a tour of the Ypres Salient, when orders to entrain for Bethune arrived.

The division was formed at the end of 1914 from battalions recalled from stations in India, Singapore and Egypt. In the new year men found themselves bound for France and the Ypres Salient. Although the officers and men were used to a completely different style of warfare, they proved their worthiness during the Second Battle of Ypres in April. The Division held the east face of the Salient when the Germans used gas for the first time on 22 April. Major-General Bulfin's command remained in line throughout the five week battle and became increasingly involved as the fighting developed. Many battalions were virtually annihilated during the later stages of the battle, and by the end of May the Division had suffered over 15,500 casualties.

Most of the men travelling south were reservists, recalled as replacements, and for them it would be their first battle: a battle where there would be no opportunities for well planned attacks, only a grim struggle for survival.

85 Brigade takes over Hohenzollern Redoubt

Around 1.00pm on 27 September, 85 Brigade arrived at Vermelles. Almost immediately Brigadier-General Cecil Pereira was instructed to move his Brigade forward to take over Fosse 8 and the Dump. However, before he could pass on the order, the news that Fosse 8 had been lost arrived. Pereira's men were now needed to secure Hohenzollen Redoubt, before it too fell into German hands. Even before the 2nd East Surreys and the 3rd Royal Fusiliers had started to move, events overtook Brigadier-General Pereira, and his orders were revised for a second time. The new plan called for the 3rd Royal Fusiliers to occupy the Redoubt while half of the 2nd Buffs reinforced Big Willie Trench. As described in the Buffs war diary, the approach march was fraught with difficulty:

> *General PEREIRA and Captain Flower (brigade major) accompanied the BUFFS. The communicating trenches were so congested with troops that the BUFFS quitted them and reached their appointed positions being shelled heavily en route. On arrival a platoon of 'D' Company charged the enemy and accounted for a score. Captain FLOWER was wounded. About this time General PEREIRA was wounded.*

Meanwhile Lieutenant-Colonel Roberts, the Royal Fusiliers CO, had gone forward alone to seek Brigadier-General Jelf. Major Baker was left to supervise the occupation of the Redoubt, an operation that took six hours to complete. It was hoped that the 2nd East Surreys would occupy Little Willie Trench and drive any Germans before them. Once again the approach march turned out to be a grim ordeal. One of A Company's officers described the journey to the regimental historian:

> *Second Lieutenant Woodyear reconnoitred the ground and trench on our left, as our orders were to clear 'Little Willie' of the enemy, who was supposed to be cut off at each end of the trench. This, however, proved not to be the case. Second Lieutenant Woodyear found there was a good length of trench unoccupied. So the company advanced in single file along the right side of the trench, i.e. the north-western face of the Redoubt. Presently we came under fire, and a few men were hit, so we got down in the trench. We then moved farther along the trench until we came to a barrier. After placing sentries along the trench and at the barrier, we took a sneak party beyond the barrier and crept round the traverses to see if the further part of the trench was occupied. We could tell that we were now at close quarters from the rifle fire, the flashes appeared to be thirty yards away.*

As soon as the East Surreys arrived in front of Little Willie, Lieutenant-Colonel Montague-Bates immediately ordered a two-pronged attack. A Company would bomb along Little Willie from the direction of the redoubt while B Company approached via New Trench. Neither group could make any progress, and the East Surreys had to be content with holding the old front line.

While 85 Brigade struggled to find its way onto the Redoubt, steps were under way to take possession of the Dump. Whoever occupied the slagheap held the key to the Fosse 8 position. General Gough recognised this, and planned to conduct a surprise attack under cover of darkness. With 85 Brigade fully occupied, the task fell to the 1st Royal Berkshires, a Battalion from Carter's Force, the makeshift Brigade 'borrowed' from 2nd Division.

The approach to the objective was long and arduous, with many trenches and belts of barbed wire to cross. As the Berkshires picked their way across the battlefield they were soon discovered, as the war diary describes:

> *Owing to the bright moonlight the enemy saw us advancing. When we were 400 yards from our objective they put up Very lights and kept a continuous fire on us from our right front - this*

Trench map covering Hohenzollern Redoubt and the Dump.

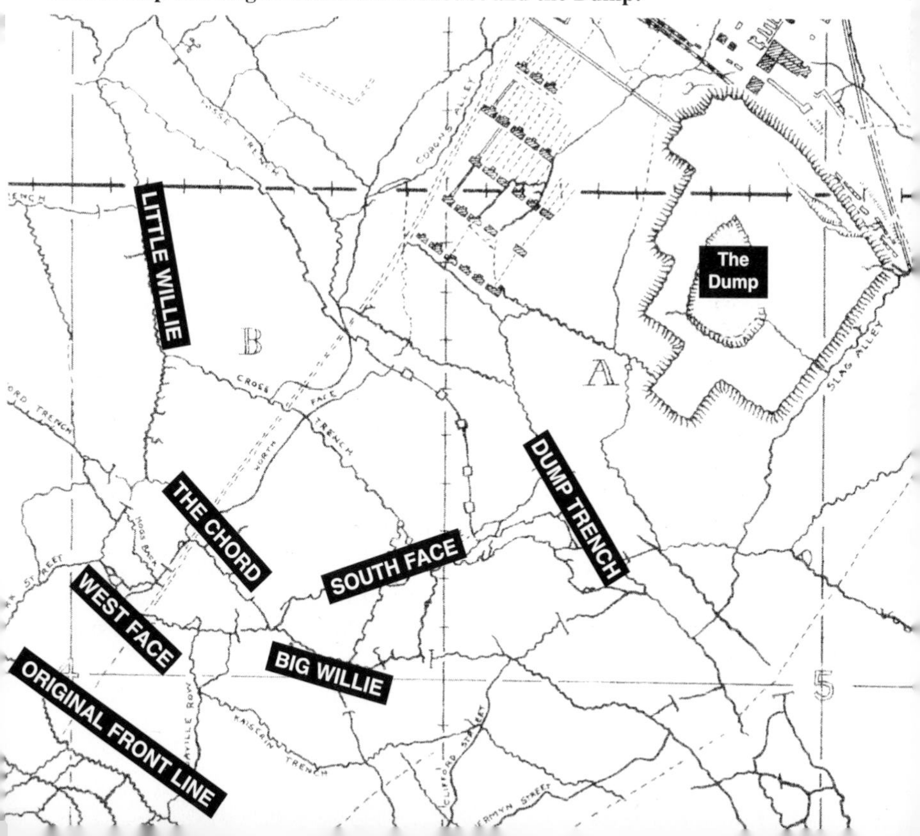

2/Lt. Turner bombing his way along Slag Alley.

grew heavier as we got nearer

The Berkshires pushed on to the foot of the Dump despite heavy losses, but they could not establish a foothold on the summit. Every time Major Bird's men climbed the steep slopes, the Germans threw dozens of bombs down. The depleted Battalion was forced to take cover in Dump Trench, but before they could reorganise the Germans counterattacked down Slag Alley. For a time it appeared as though the Berkshires would be driven out into the open. At a crucial moment Second Lieutenant Alexander Buller Turner volunteered to counterattack:

Second-Lieutenant Alexander Turner VC.

2nd Lieut. A B Turner single-handedly bombed down a German communications trench, driving the enemy before him a distance of over 150 yards. During the whole of this period the Germans were throwing bombs at Second Lieutenant Turner. While performing this very gallant act he was mortally wounded.

Although it was impossible to hold onto the captured trench, Turner's actions had saved the Battalion and allowed it retain a valuable position. With the Germans falling back, Lieutenant-Colonel Carter ordered D Company and half of C Company forward. The small force charged up the slopes of slagheap in a last desperate attempt to take it. Showers of bombs met the Berkshires as they climbed, forcing them to retire back to Dump Trench for a second time.

The Berkshires lost nearly three hundred men. Their CO, Major Bird, had been wounded and Captain Maurice Radford DSO, his second in command, lay dead. Second Lieutenant Turner died of his wounds on 1 October and was buried at Choques Casualty Clearing Station. Alexander Turner's Victoria Cross was the second of three awarded to members of his family over the years. His middle name, 'Buller', came from General Sir Redvers Henry Buller who received the Victoria Cross in 1879 during the Zulu War. In 1942 Alexander's younger brother, Victor, gained the award in North Africa.

Dawn on the 28th found 85 Brigade holding a foothold on the Redoubt, while the Germans still held Little Willie Trench to the west and the Dump to the east. It had been hoped that the Brigade would be in a position to attack the Dump at dawn. The plan directed the 2nd Buffs to advance from Dump Trench onto the summit of the slagheap, while the 3rd Middlesex bombed along South Face Trench. However, delays in getting the men in position meant that zero hour was postponed until 9.30am. The relief of Dump Trench in full view of the Germans on the slagheap was a dangerous operation. The Buffs' war diary graphically illustrates the difficult conditions;

> *.... the Companies filed up the trenches and suffered many casualties en route from shell fire. The congested state of the trenches due to dead, wounded and units waiting to be relieved admitted very slow progress. One position whence one Coy was to attack was in possession of the enemy, and these circumstances prevented the companies taking up their approximate positions until after 10.00am*

The supporting barrage had already ended at 9.30am and the Buffs knew that the element of surprise had been lost. Fully alerted to the impending attack the Germans trained every available machine-gun on the jumping off trench. At 10.00am the Buffs climbed into the open and advanced as ordered:

> *'B' and 'C' Coys followed by 'A' Coy charged across the open and were greeted with the fire from machine-guns massed on either flank, also shell and rifle fire. Eleven machine-guns, at least, were afterwards counted firing from the Miners' Cottages and Slag Alley. 'B' and 'C' Coys - every man cheering - gained the edge of the DUMP and, clambering up the crumbling slopes of the 30 foot high DUMP gained the summit.*

The DUMP was then plastered with shells of all descriptions both from our own guns and those of the enemy and the attack was broken. The Coys crossed the large expanse of the DUMP summit and attempted to reach the enemy in the trenches at the foot. It was a hopeless task and those who attempted it were shot or grenaded. The Coys reformed and returned to the original trenches, leaving over 100 men killed or wounded on the DUMP.

Meanwhile, the 3rd Middlesex had made good progress to begin with, working their way along South Face Trench before turning left into Dump Trench. However, before long they ran out of bombs and found themselves trapped. The war diary illustrates how difficult it was to withdraw from a congested trench:

Considerable progress was made when bombs ran out and urgent appeals were made for more. The Battalion then began to suffer considerable casualties from a heavy attack with bombs by the enemy. The narrow trench then became congested with wounded, men of other units who were relieved and on their way out of the trench and also the Buffs who had to give way on our

Moving troops along narrow trenches was extremely difficult. IWM Q28982

The Dump viewed from the original front line, Big Willie and Dump Trench can be seen. IWM - 42190

> *right. The C.O. then gave the order to withdraw slowly. This operation was most difficult, the trench being a narrow one and seven feet deep. We were enfiladed on both sides by M.G. fire and it was impossible to show a head over the parapet*

Lieutenant-Colonel George Neale was killed as the Battalion withdrew. Taking advantage of the Middlesexs' plight, the German bombers counterattacked and entered Dump Trench, driving a wedge between the two battalions. Eventually the Germans were stopped and while the bombing continued barricades were built.

Throughout the day and overnight the bombing contest continued. Lieutenant W T Williams led the defence on the Buffs side of the gap in appalling conditions:

> *As night fell the rain commenced again and never ceased. Shell and rifle fire slackened but the bomb throwing was stronger than ever. Our bomb throwers were nearly all killed or wounded and others were borrowed from neighbouring units. Owing to the rain the fuses were damp, matches gave out, and the only way to light the fuses was by means of keeping cigarettes alight. The organisation of the enemy bomb throwers was astounding. He threw at least five bombs to our one and of a much more powerful description. During the night every endeavour was made to get in the wounded. Neither rations nor water were obtainable. Attempts were made to dig in but the mud rendered it a slow and laborious task. Dawn showed no cessation in the bomb throwing.*

Elsewhere on 85 Brigade front the fighting had died down as both sides attempted to consolidate their positions. Even so the shelling continued unabated and in many places the trenches hardly existed.

The following day, the 29th, heavy rain added to the miseries of the men on the Redoubt. Trenches turned into drainage channels, and movement all but stopped in the quagmire. In many cases the mud rendered rifles useless. The British-made bombs often failed to work in the damp conditions, putting 85 Brigade at a severe disadvantage in close quarter fighting.

It had been the intention to relieve the 2nd Buffs from Dump Trench with the 1st York and Lancasters, from 83 Brigade, on the night of the 29th. At 3.00am A and B Companies set off along Central Boyau. Before long they were forced to halt by scores of wounded men who were trying to make their way back to safety along the narrow trench. Finding their guides to be of little use, Captain Forster and Captain Buckley went ahead in frustration to try and make contact with the Buffs. By the time they returned dawn was approaching, and the York and Lancaster men faced the unenviable task of taking over a contested sector in daylight. German observers on top of the Dump watched as the York and Lancasters approached, and, sensing an opportunity, reported the impending relief. The local commander acted quickly, ordering a bombing raid to take advantage of the situation. The chaos that followed is detailed in the York and Lancasters war diary:

> *About 6am A Company advanced through BIG WILLIE and two platoons had entered the advance trench when the Germans commenced a strong bomb attack on the left flank. The Buffs meanwhile, were filing out and the trenches were very congested. The order was given by the adjutant of the Buffs to 'About turn', but this was almost impossible owing to the congestion, although No. 4 Platoon was able to file into an empty trench to allow the Buffs to pass. Captain Buckley, in response to a request for bombs, led the bombers of 'B' Company over the top and delivered an attack, returning when the supply of bombs was exhausted. The wounded passing down the trench made the trench more congested still and the order was given to charge. The charge was led by Major Robertson and Captain Forster and was successful in preventing the Germans coming over the top and also drove them back along their trench.*

Machine-guns on the Dump opened fire, killing and wounding many, including all of A Company's officers. The charge did manage to subdue the Germans, forcing their bomb squads to withdraw.

However, the Brigade's troubles were far from over. A second bomb attack along South Face Trench forced the 3rd Middlesex to retire to West Face Trench. When news of the reversal filtered through to the

Private Samuel Harvey VC.

York and Lancasters, Lieutenant Coles, B Company's CO, went in search of the Middlesex. Instead all he found was a long section of unoccupied trench. In the confusion part of Big Willie Trench had been evacuated, leaving the 1st York and Lancasters left flank exposed. Lieutenant Bates was immediately sent for to reoccupy the empty trench, and war diary relates what Bates' party discovered:

The Germans who had evidently crept up an unused communications trench were established in BIG WILLIE with a supply of bombs. The party withdrew to report and ordered to return with bombs In the meantime the Germans had advanced up the trench slowly and were assisted by gas fumes which emanated from a burning mop shaped apparatus which had been placed on our parapet.

From their lodgement in Big Willie Trench, the Germans began to bomb down the York and Lancaster's line forcing them to retire. Bomb supplies were running low and, with the redoubt in German hands, it was impossible to obtain any from that direction. The 2nd East Yorkshire's bomb squad came to the rescue and, under the leadership of Second Lieutenant Frere, the Germans were checked.

For the next six hours the bomb fight continued, and the York and Lancaster's expended hundreds of bombs. Private Samuel Harvey saw to it that his comrades did not run out.

When more bombs were urgently required Harvey volunteered to fetch them. The communication trench was blocked with wounded and reinforcements, and he went backwards and forwards across the open and succeeded in bringing up no less than thirty boxes of bombs before he was wounded in the head. It was mainly due to Harvey's bravery that the enemy was eventually driven back.

Harvey was awarded the Victoria Cross. It appears that he never fully recovered from his head injury and for the rest of his life he wandered from job to job. Samuel Harvey died a pauper in 1960 and although he was afforded a full military funeral he was buried in an unmarked communal grave.

While the fighting had been raging in Dump Trench and Big Willie, the 2nd East Surrey's had been subjected to a number of attacks. A series of bomb attacks along Little Willie Trench had threatened to drive Second Lieutenant Jameson's bomb squad back. The Germans were eventually halted when Second Lieutenant Alfred Fleming-

Sandes arrived with a fresh supply of bombs.

The 3rd Royal Fusiliers, holding the centre of Hohenzollern Redoubt fared no better. As the day wore on the Battalion's grip on the redoubt was being slowly eroded. Their war diary gives a detailed summary of the fighting:

> *On the morning of the 29th the German bombers attacked Little Willie and North Face and after a heavy fight were only kept out by No 4 coming up in support of the E. Surreys. No 2 Company also advanced to straighten up the line, but could not go far as the right was turned there by the Germans bombing down South Face. Shelling was fairly heavy that afternoon and the heaviest attack of all took place down South Face and the Middlesex evacuated Big Willie, leaving the flank of No. 2 Coy in the air. The Germans bombed down Western Face driving No 2 Coy back to almost the head of the communications trench leading from the supports.*

Second-Lieutenant Alfred Fleming-Sandes VC.

'C' Company of the York and Lancaster's made an impromptu counterattack to try and restore the

Second-Lieutenant Alfred Fleming-Sandes VC

situation:

At 5pm there was a sudden panic in the Redoubt and about 50 men rushed over the top into our trench. The order was given to fix bayonets. About 5.30pm Captain Lucas gave the order to charge. The left flank put out of action a bombing party which was stationed at the corner of the Redoubt and a communication trench.

Although Lucas' attempt failed to clear the Redoubt, it did manage to give the Royal Fusiliers breathing space.

When the Fusiliers started to withdraw from the Redoubt, the East Surreys began to waver. Second Lieutenant Fleming-Sandes climbed out onto the parapet and hurled bombs at the Germans in Little Willie Trench, driving them back. When a rifle bullet shattered his right arm Fleming-Sandes continued to use his left arm, only stopping when a second bullet seriously wounded him in the face. Inspired by his bravery the East Surrey held Little Willie Trench. Second Lieutenant Alfred Fleming-Sandes Victoria Cross was gazetted seven weeks later. His wound took months to heal and he eventually returned to active service in 1918. After the war Fleming-Sandes emigrated to Egypt, ultimately rising to the rank of Provincial Judge in the Sudan Civil Service. During the Second World War he played an active role in the Sudan Auxilary Defence Force. Fleming-Sandes eventually retired in 1944 and returned to England; he died in 1961, a few weeks before his 67th birthday.

As darkness fell across the Redoubt, No 2 Company and No 4 Company of the 3rd Royal Fusiliers drove the Germans out of Big Willie and Western Face. Although some order had been restored, 85 Brigade's hold on the Redoubt was slowly diminishing.

Throughout the day the 2nd East Yorkshires' bomb squads had been present in Big Willie. Time after time Second Lieutenants Frere and Gatrell saved the situation, working ceaselessly to keep the Germans at bay. That night the East Yorkshires CO sent a message to Brigade. Its tone displays the disgust shown by many at the quality and quantity of bombs being supplied:

Our bombers have suffered severely during the day, repulsed counter attacks from Slag Alley and direction of Point 35 on behalf of other battalions and are now so reduced that they are only able to hold the ground gained. The second class bombs sent today have helped largely in producing these casualties. I shall require at least 1,500 first class grenades before moving as my stock has nearly run out. The Germans appear to have an immense reserve and succeed always in producing bombs when our own are finished.

Although shelling and bombing continued throughout the 30th neither side managed to gain any ground. As darkness fell the men of 85 Brigade began to file out of the trenches, exhausted after three days of continuous fighting.

While 85 Brigade fought for its life on the redoubt, the remainder of Brigadier-General Hurdis Ravenshaw's 83 Brigade held the line to the east. The 2nd King's Own occupied Quarry Trench, under 22 Brigade's command. Meanwhile, the 2nd East Yorkshires held the sector opposite the Quarries. Ravenshaw's men consolidating the line and, despite constant shelling and probing bombing attacks, managed to improve their positions; deepening trenches, strengthening parapets and building barricades. On the night of 2 October Ravenshaw handed over a substantially improved sector to the Guards Division.

Chapter Nine

28th DIVISION CONTINUES ON THE REDOUBT

84 Brigade

With 85 Brigade exhausted, Brigadier-General Tom Pearse's Brigade prepared for the arduous task of taking over the front line. Reports concerning the situation on the redoubt were confusing. Some optimistically stated that both Fosse Trench and Dump Trench were held, others gave the impression that 85 Brigade had been forced back to the original front line. In reality, as the sun set on 30 September, the British occupied the West Face of the Redoubt and Big Willie Trench. The Germans controlled most of Little Willie Trench, threatening the north flank of the redoubt. Barricades in North and South Face and the communication trenches leading towards Fosse 8, were keeping the Germans at bay for the time being. It was intended that Pearse's fresh brigade would be able to take up the offensive and secure Hohenzollern Redoubt.

Hohenzollern Redoubt before the German attack on 3 October. The British only hold West Face and part of Big Willie Trench.

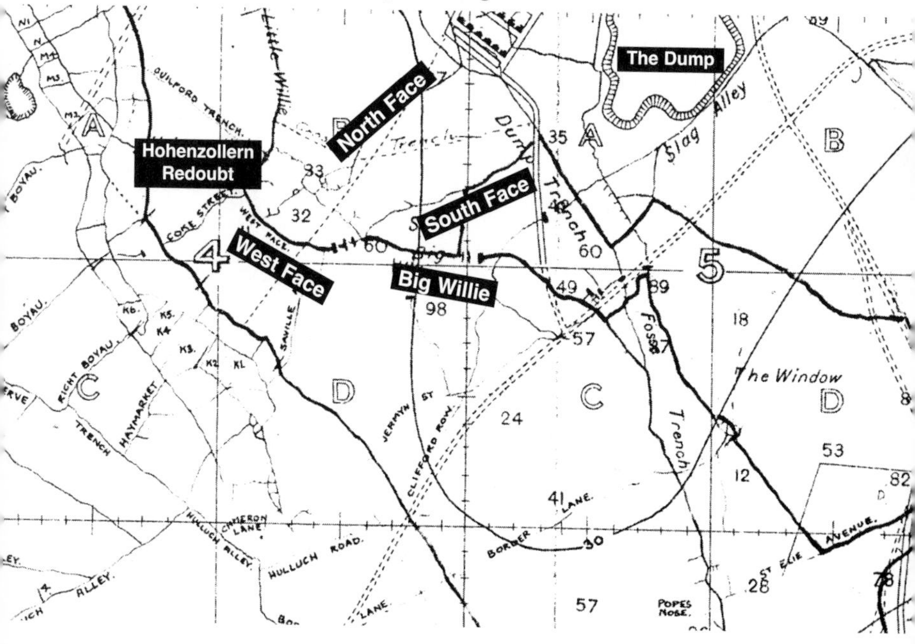

The process of relieving 85 Brigade lasted all night. With only two guides to lead the entire Brigade through the maze of trenches, it is not surprising that some companies lost their way. Under cover of darkness, the 1st Welch had taken over the old front line opposite Little Willie Trench, on the left of the Brigade. Meanwhile, the 2nd Cheshires had occupied the West Face of the redoubt unscathed.

At first light the Northumberland Fusiliers were still in the process of taking over Big Willie Trench on the right of the brigade. As they moved up the trenches, German observers watched every move from the summit of the Dump. They were alerted when some of the York and Lancaster men, anxious to get back to the rear, climbed out of the trench and ran to safety. For a second time the German sentries sensed that a relief was in progress. Before the Northumberland Fusiliers had a chance to settle in, a bomb squad crept down South Face Trench. When they reached the junction of Big Willie and West Face, the bombers divided into two. One worked its way west, driving 'D' Company of the Fusiliers back along West Face. The second group moved east down Big Willie Trench, capturing one hundred metres from 'C' Company. After a desperate struggle both bombing teams were stopped and barricades were built to contain them. It did however, leave the Fusiliers spilt in two, with no way of communicating between

A working party map; new trenches have appeared, connecting Big Willie to the British trenches.

the two halves; an extremely awkward position.

The setback was an embarrassment to Brigadier-General Pearse, for it effectively split his front in two. Brigade headquarters soon issued orders to the Fusiliers, instructing them to reunite the two halves of its command. All day 'C' and 'D' companies tried to push the Germans out of Big Willie. Major Charles Armstrong, the CO, and Lieutenant Ivan Gilchrist, the adjutant, died in the bomb engagement and Captain Lamb was severely wounded. A chronic shortage of bombs hampered the Fusiliers throughout the day. Only when the 2nd Cheshires bombers came to their assistance around dusk could D Company make any headway, eventually retaking fifty metres of trench.

Otherwise 84 Brigade was allowed to settle in and adjust to its new positions, although the endless bombardment destroyed men and trenches alike. In places the troops were forced to shelter in shallow ditches no more than a metre deep.

Brigadier-General Pearse had been given orders to attack that night, to improve his hold on the German trenches. The plan was to clear Little Willie Trench and secure the Redoubt with two battalions. There would be no artillery bombardment; instead it was hoped that the objectives could be taken by surprise, a bold yet risky scheme. On the left the 1st Welch would take Little Willie and their instructions were simple:

> *Precisely at 8pm, climb over the parapet. Move forward in perfect silence, move in quick time, keep line.*

On the right, No 3 and No 4 Companies of the 2nd Cheshires were to advance across the Redoubt, again they were to use stealth to overrun the Germans. They were to take a new trench known as The Chord, described in their war diary as *"a strong trench running north to south across the Hohenzollern Redoubt".*

The Cheshires' positions were far from ideal from which to launch an attack from. In places their jumping off trench, the West Face of the Redoubt, was no more than knee deep. The Germans held both ends of the trench, kept at bay behind barricades. Bringing the assault troops into position was a long and laborious task. They had to share a single trench with the companies they were replacing. Consequently the relief, which began when darkness fell, took far longer than anticipated. Yet again orders from division and above bore no relation to the conditions at the front. Zero hour was eventually postponed until midnight to give the men time to assemble.

In accordance with their orders, the Welsh crept over the parapet and advanced silently towards Little Willie Trench. With only one hundred metres to go they were spotted, and the alarm raised. Reacting swiftly, the Germans opened fire, as reported in the Welsh's war diary:

> *The commanding officer's voice rang out 'Forward 41st - Get at 'em Welsh'. In twenty seconds there were 250 men and a proportion of the officers on the floor. The remainder were in the trench bayoneting those in the trench and firing at the retreating Prussian Guards.*

Although Lieutenant-Colonel Hoggan's men had captured a large section of Little Willie Trench, their success left them in a predicament. The company on the right had lost touch with the rest of the Battalion, leaving a section of trench in the middle of the Welsh's line in German control. Meanwhile, the left of the Battalion only held part of Little Willie. Half a dozen bays at the north end were still in German hands, leaving them in an excellent position to strike at the Welsh's flank. To make matters worse, there was no communications trench connecting Little Willie Trench to the support trenches. The Welsh were cut off. A few men managed to bring bombs and ammunition over the top under cover of darkness, but the journeys ceased at daybreak. All through the night the 1st Welch and the 6th Welch frantically dug their way towards each other to form a link.

On the redoubt, the Cheshires managed to make progress and captured what they thought was the Chord. They were in fact mistaken, for amongst the maze of ditches and shell holes it was impossible to tell where the trench started or finished. Although Brigade wanted the Chord, Major Roddy advised against further attacks. His men were fully employed trying to consolidate the ground they had taken.

The following day the Germans relentlessly pounded the Redoubt

Due to endless shelling trenches were reduced to shallow ditches by the later stages of the battle. IWM - Q28974

and Little Willie with trench mortars. The effects of this devastating weapon in the shallow trenches is summarised in the 1st Welch war diary:

> *The enemy then opened with Minenwerfer shell - this is what soldiers call 'Sausage Up'. The shell, having reached the distance it is regulated for, drops perpendicularly down and can be seen all the way down and can be dodged. The men were now so congested that is was impossible to get out of the way. When one lands in the trench six men in the vicinity disappear.*

The Welsh were in a terrible situation, isolated on all sides. By 10.00am their bomb supply had been exhausted, leaving them virtually powerless to stop counterattacks. At 2.30pm there was a glimmer of hope when the communications trench was completed. It was, however, too late. A fierce bombing attack struck the 1st Welch before they could remove the wounded and reorganise. Without bombs to reply the Welsh stood no chance, and Little Willie Trench fell into German hands. Major Arthur Hobbs was last seen leading a bayonet charge through a shower of grenades. Although some managed to escape down the new communications trench, many wounded were left behind during the chaotic withdrawal. The 1/6th Welch managed to prevent the German pursuit along New Trench, although Lieutenant-Colonel Lord Ninian Crichton-Stuart, their commanding officer, was killed leading the defence.

Later that afternoon, Brigadier-General Pearse instructed the 1st Suffolks to retake Little Willie. The Battalion set off at 7.00pm along Central Boyau Trench, leaving little more than an hour to get into position. As the head of the column approached the front line, they found the way forward blocked. With no alternative route available, the Suffolks were forced to leave the trenches to get to their allotted position. In the darkness, Second Lieutenant Gates and D Company became lost amongst the network of trenches. To compensate for the delay, brigade delayed zero hour, first to 10.30pm and then to midnight. With fifteen minutes to go A Company were only just entering the jumping off trench and D Company were nowhere to be seen. A final plea to postpone the attack was refused by Brigade; there was no turning back. The Suffolks' war diary graphically describes the fiasco that followed:

> *Orders were then given by Major Sinclair-Thompson to get the men out of the trenches and line up in two lines, C and D in the front line from left to right and covered off by A and B Coys, OC B Coy was ordered to take place of D Coy, whose men could*

not be found. A Coy moved off before the other companies were ready, and the attack of the other three companies, inclined to the right. The attack failed.

The following morning the Germans struck a devastating blow from the direction of Little Willie They took the few remaining Welsh by surprise, driving them back towards the Redoubt. Next came the 2nd Cheshires, and they too were driven back, leaving the Chord and West Face in German hands:

The enemy broke through part of the trench occupied by the 1st Welch on our left flank and advanced with great rapidity, throwing hundreds of bombs, their bombers being supported by machine guns and riflemen. The attack came as a complete surprise.

The Cheshires were forced to run across the open to the British trenches, and many, including Major Arthur Hill and Captain Frank Lloyd, were shot down.

Relentlessly, the Germans pushed on, taking advantage of the confusion they had caused. Next in line was the isolated company of Northumberland Fusiliers at the end of South Face;

.......the grenades which were very large, were well thrown, came down in a constant hail breaking down all resistance and killing all before it.

Trench fighting was a confused, congested affair. A ready supply of reliable bombs was essential to keep the opposition at bay. IWM - Q28972

With Germans behind them, manning the barricade at the head of South Face, D Company were trapped. They had no choice but to make a run for it over the top; only twenty-six under Captain Freeman made it to safety. The Germans were eventually brought to a halt by C Company of the Northumberland Fusiliers at the head of Big Willie Trench.

In no time at all Hohenzollern Redoubt had fallen; the only trench still in British hands was the section of Big Willie held by the Northumberland Fusiliers. The attack was a complete contrast to the fumbling efforts made the previous nights. By employing superior tactics and with the aid of a constant supply of reliable bombs, the Germans had illustrated how it was possible to break the deadlock. The British had a lot to learn about trench warfare. Brigadier-General Pearse's Brigade was a spent force and preparations to replace it were underway.

83 Brigade on the Redoubt

With the Redoubt and Little Willie in German hands, 28th Division was for the most part back in the old British front line. Major General Bulfin was determined to restore the position before he handed it over and within hours of the German attack, orders were issued for a counterattack designed to retake both Little Willie Trench and the whole of the Redoubt.

Although Brigadier-General Ravenshaw's men had just spent four days improving the line between the Dump and Hulluch Quarries, there was little time to rest. Ravenshaw's brigade had only just taken over the front when the orders arrived. Three battalions would carry out a conventional attack, over the top, at 4.15am. The 1st KOYLIs and the 2nd East Yorkshires would charge onto the redoubt while the 2nd King's Own captured and consolidated Big Willie Trench. It was hoped that the Germans could be taken by surprise under cover of darkness; it was a plan that had failed to work the previous two nights.

Many officers had deep reservations; there was no time to reconnoitre the ground and prepare jumping off positions. They would be advancing blind into a fiercely contested maze of trenches. Even so they prepared as well as they could, spending the hours of darkness taking over the front line from 84 Brigade.

At 4.15am the first two waves of the 1st KOYLIs crept over the top and lay down thirty yards in front of their trench. The third wave did the same fifteen minutes later. It was hoped that in doing so the whole battalion could move together towards the German trenches. The 2nd

East Yorkshires deployed in the same manner, Captain Wilson's B Company moving out at 4.20am. The third battalion, the 2nd King's Own, would attempt to secure the junction of West Face and Big Willie Trench by bombing.

In the minutes leading up to zero hour all were concerned by the apparent lack of artillery support. Both the 1st KOYLI and East Yorkshire war diaries are adamant that there was none. The artillery diaries disagree. Either way, whatever shelling took place had no effect on the Germans. As the waves of men rose to advance a heavy fire opened up. Half of the men in the KOYLIs first wave, were hit almost immediately and the rest faltered. Captain the Honourable H A Law, with the second wave, pushed forward in vain. In the time it took to advance one hundred metres, 180 men had fallen. The East Yorkshires suffered a similar fate; B Company, under Captain Wilson, lost two thirds of its number in a couple of minutes. D Company was delayed in the congested trenches and by the time they were ready to advance it was all over. Meanwhile, the 2nd King's Own attack was met by heavy crossfire directed from South Face and Dump Trench. To make matters worse the direction of the assault was incorrect. Yet again the German machine-guns stopped the attack in a few minutes.

28th Division's final attempt to secure the Redoubt was a hurried, ill-conceived plan and many were disgusted by it. Lieutenant-Colonel Blake, the 2nd East Yorkshires CO, pulled no punches when he completed his battalion war diary:

I attribute the failure of this attack to following causes:

(i) No Artillery bombardment

(ii) Complete lack of element of surprise. The Germans were well prepared, and had not been in the slightest shaken by the desultory shelling that had taken place throughout the day.

(iii) The Germans had been digging in during the day previous, and had thoroughly improved their trenches.

(iv) The relief the day before did not finish until 7pm. Company officers had only very indistinct idea of the trenches they were occupying, and none at all of the positions they were to attack.

That night the Guards Division relieved Bulfin's men. In a week his Division had suffered over 3,200 casualties. Bulfin was invalided home a week later, drained by the fighting on Hohenzollen Redoubt.

GUARDS DIVISION

The loss of Hohenzollen Redoubt left First Army's flank in a dangerous position, and General Haig was anxious to recover both Fosse 8 and Hulluch Quarries before winter arrived. On the night of 4 October Lieutenant-General Richard Haking, GOC XI Corps, took over responsibility for the line facing Hohenzollen and the Quarries, with instructions to prepare for an attack as soon as possible. For a second time gas was to be used, accompanied by smoke. It was

Men from B Company of the 1st Scots Guards in Big Willie Trench.
IWM - Q17390

proposed to use the Guards Division (which had just suffered a bloody defeat on IV Corps front at Loos) to capture the Redoubt. A fresh formation, Major-General Scotts' 12th (Eastern) Division would take the Quarries. However, both Divisions faced a great deal of work before the attack could be launched.

New assembly trenches and gas emplacements were needed, and the Guardsmen eventually carried 120 gas cylinders into position. All the work had to be carried out at night under incessant shellfire, and delays forced General Haig to postpone the attack until 9 October. The work was arduous and one particular incident on the 6th incensed the 1st Coldstream Guards:

> *Nothing much occurred except our losing two men killed and one Sergeant wounded from our own guns. Vigorous protest. Result next day a score of gunners are detailed to stay as FOO's* [Forward Observation Officers]. *They were put in the front trench and this had a magic effect on the shooting of our guns.*

Meanwhile, the Germans had not been idle, and on the afternoon of the 8th they struck. Rather than attacking over the top, they preferred to attack along the trenches. The history of the 57th Regiment illustrates how advanced German bombing tactics were at this stage in the war:

> *About 4.30pm the barricades of the saps were broken down and the attack began. At the head of each of the two columns that were to storm along the saps was a strong party of bombers, followed by men carrying filled sandbags ready to make a barricade at once whenever necessary. Behind there was a detachment with rifles and hand grenades who were to search*

Guards Division's dispositions during the German attack on 8 October.

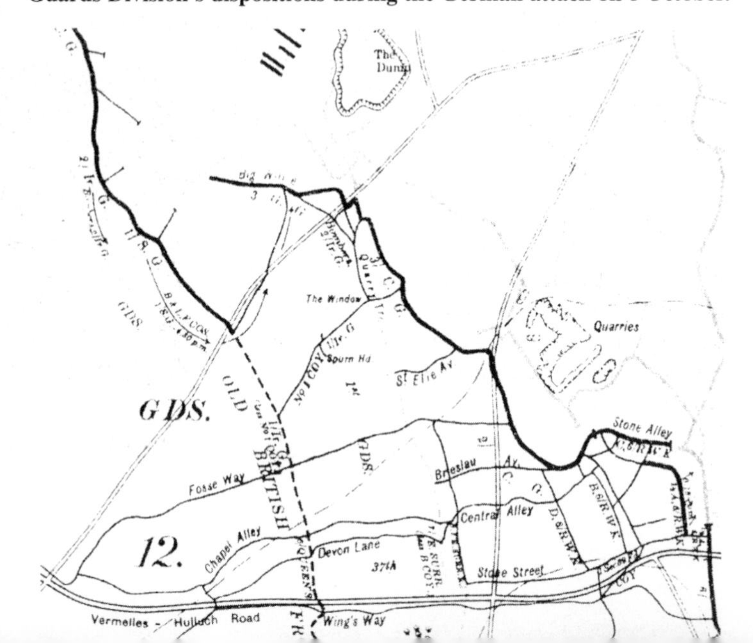

and clear any enemy dug-outs and defend barricades. At the tail of the column were reserve bombers for replacing casualties in the front bombing party.

Although most of the attacks were repulsed, the Germans did manage to drive the 3rd Grenadier Guards back down Big Willie Trench:

The enemy bombers rushed our left flank and came bombing down the line. They surprised and surrounded our own bombers killing most of them, including Lieutenant Anson. A machine-gun crew, commanded by Lieutenant Robert Williams from the Battalion, were also killed and three successive machine-gun Sergeants. The two companies who occupied the finger, Numbers 2 and 3, were ordered to retire down the communication trench and make way for bombs and bombers who were hurried up from the support companies.

A section of the 3rd Coldstream Guards led by Lance-Sergeant Oliver Brooks and six bombers were instrumental in thwarting the Germans. Brooks' party began to bomb their way forward, eventually retaking over two hundred metres of Big Willie Trench. As reported in the Battalion war diary they wanted to go further;

....so confident were the bombing party that they were eager to continue operations and invade the German lines ....

For their determined counterattack the bombers were rewarded with the Distinguished Conduct Medal. Brooks received the ultimate reward for leading the group, the Victoria Cross. He was wounded twelve months later on the Somme, and when he recovered became a bombing instructor. Olly Brooks died in Windsor in 1940.

Although the Germans had failed to capture any territory, they had managed to disrupt General Haig's plans for an attack on the 9th. Instead First Army set zero hour for 2.00pm on 13th October. The Guards continued their work preparing the front line, but they would not now be called upon to strike at the Redoubt. They were in no fit state to conduct an attack and their place would be taken by the 46th (North Midland) Division. The division had been in France since March, when it had been proud to be the first territorial formation on French soil. It spent the next six months in the Ypres Salient, but the attack on the Redoubt would be its first major battle - and one it would not forget.

Lance-Sergeant Oliver Brooks VC

46th (NORTH MIDLAND) DIVISION

Major-General the Honourable Edward Montagu-Stuart-Wortley had wanted to employ bombing tactics to capture Fosse 8 and the Redoubt. He was, however, over-ruled and his revised plan ordered 138 Brigade to attack the Redoubt head on, advancing over the top. Continuing past Fosse Trench, the men would advance through the Corons and retake the pithead buildings. Meanwhile, 137 Brigade would advance from Big Willie and the trenches behind, across Dump Trench. The troops would then pass to the east of the slagheap, linking with 138 Brigade on the far side of the Dump. Simultaneously, bombing parties would worm their way forward, securing the maze of trenches ready for consolidation.

There was a serious attempt to familiarise the troops with the battlefield. Before the battle, divisional staff built a large-scale plan of the objective at their headquarters. Using bricks, coal and other materials to hand, they created a three-dimensional model for everyone to study. The officers were also given a 'guided tour' of the trenches to help them get accustomed with the terrain.

The attack was to be preceded by gas, although it was acknowledged that there was not enough to incapacitate the Germans. Instead First Army hoped that the smell of gas in the air would shake

46th Division's plan of attack with brigade objectives outlined.

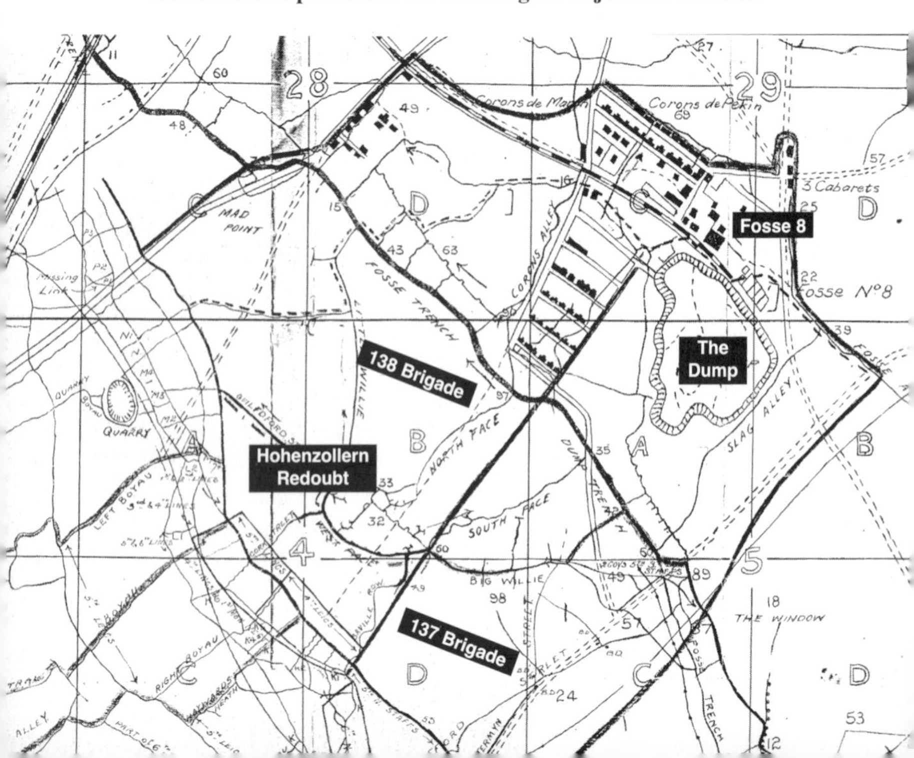

the Germans' morale. The gas programme was to last for one hour as follows:

0-50 Minutes: *Run two cylinders until empty, then release one cylinder. Finally release two cylinders*

50-60 Minutes: *Turn off gas, switch to smoke using mortars, candles and grenades.*

This time there was no time, or room, to dig a 'gas trench' and the assault troops had to share the trench with the Special Brigade. The congestion caused problems as reported in 138 Brigade's war diary:

> *Owing to a large amount of room taken up in front trench by the gas cylinders and fittings, and to the risk of gas poisoning in the event of a cylinder being destroyed by the enemy's fire, I thinned out the ranks there to those for the first and second lines, placing the third and fourth lines in the first supporting line ....*

Corporal James Dawson VC

At noon the artillery bombardment began and, although the Germans responded feebly, an occasional shell managed to cause mayhem. Disaster struck on 138 Brigade's front when shrapnel damaged a number of gas cylinders. Corporal James Dawson, serving with 187th Company RE (Special Brigade), braved the bullets and climbed onto the parapet to assess the situation. From this exposed position he was able to direct the assault troops away from the affected area, saving many from suffocation. Dawson then hauled the cylinders onto the parados and rolled them away from the trench. By emptying his pistol into the cylinders he managed to release the gas at a safe distance. Corporal Dawson's quick thinking and bravery allowed 138 Brigade to reoccupy its jumping off trench in time to attack at their appointed hour. He was awarded the Victoria Cross, which was gazetted in December 1915. Originally

Corporal Dawson rolls damaged gas cylinders away from the trenches.

Corporal Dawson had joined the 5th Scottish Rifles and was posted to France in the spring of 1915. A few weeks later he was drafted to the Special Brigade on the strength of his degree in chemistry. Dawson was wounded and invalided home the following summer. He remained with the army, serving in India and America on staff duties, until 1946, retiring with the rank of Colonel.

137 (Staffordshire) Brigade attacks the Dump

Brigadier-General Edward Feetham found it almost impossible to deploy his troops for the assault. The 1/5th North Staffordshires had to start from the old front line, three hundred metres away from Big Willie Trench, while the 1/5th South Staffordshires jumping off position was split in two. B and C Companies held part of Big Willie close to the Dump. Meanwhile, A and D Companies, along with battalion headquarters, occupied the old front line three hundred metres to the rear.

As zero hour approached, observers noted that the artillery barrage was not having the desired effect on the Germans holding the Dump. Two reports from the front line illustrate their reaction to the barrage:

The bombardment did not appear to affect the 'South Face' or the 'Dump Trench' south of G.5.a.3.5, as a great deal of sniping from these trenches took place between 12.00 noon and 2.00pm: - three of our periscopes were hit between 1.40pm and 2.00pm.

At 1.30pm I heard machine-gun fire which I found was directed onto the assembly trenches. This continued for five minutes and I at once reported to Brigade H.Q. saying that I believed the fire came from the direction of the DUMP. At 1.45pm the machine-gun fire opened again in greater volume, and I reported the fact to Brigade Headquarters, adding that many more machine-guns appeared to be firing, and that their fire came from the SOUTH FACE TRENCH and in rear of it.

Although the smoke cloud obscured the troops as they formed up, machine-gun fire from several directions scythed through the troops as they climbed out into the open. The 1/5th North Staffords, led by Lieutenant-Colonel John Knight, went forward shouting, "Forward the Potters" and "Up the Potters". The two companies on the left were virtually wiped out:

Captain Wood (D Coy) is the only officer left of the left section of the attack - he was 2nd in command of the 2nd line company. He reports that they advanced on BIG WILLIE and that he thinks some of B Coy reached this trench. Captain Wood with one man found themselves alone about sixty yards from BIG WILLIE; they got into a shell hole and walked back to the assembly trench after dark.

Captain Worthington's A Company was also cut to pieces in the first few yards and the survivors were forced to take cover in an old communications trench. C Company, suffered a similar fate. When their last officer fell, the leaderless men joined A Company. The bombing party found the communications trench blocked, and they were forced to advance over the top. Only two returned unhurt. The 1/5th North Staffordshire's sustained over five hundred casualties, most had been hit within a few yards of their own trench.

The first two companies of the 1/6th North Staffordshire's followed in support:

Under a very heavy rifle and machine-gun fire from the enemy, which accounted for the large number of casualties in the first 200 yards of the advance .... Apparently there were no Company officers left with the leading two companies and the men got grouped together and suffered heavily in consequence, particularly on the left.

Realising that the attack had failed, Lieutenant-Colonel R F Ratcliff ordered his two reserve companies to stand-fast.

The advance of the 1/5th South Staffordshires from Big Willie Trench never materialised. Devastating machine-gun fire from the Dump and South Face Trench cut B and C Companies to pieces before they had passed through their own wire. Meanwhile, the support companies advanced through the smoke screen unaware of what lay ahead:

No 7 platoon on the right of 'B' Company left the trench to form up on the parapet for the assault and was followed by No 8 and No 6. Captain Miller, commanding the company, the platoon officers of No 7 and 8 and most of No 7 platoon were almost immediately hit by enfilade machine-gun fire from the left, and the rest of the Company was withdrawn into the trench to await the arrival of the first line of the 1/5th North Staffs Regt.

Having received no message that our front line had been unable to advance and not being able to see their positions for smoke, the two companies forming the third line followed the second line and suffered very heavy casualties - 18 of all ranks from A Company and 53 from C Company survived.

The fourth line, encumbered with sandbags, barbed wire, bombs and ammunition, followed a few minutes later. They too had no idea that the attack had failed. Although the machine-guns in South Face Trench had by now switched targets to engage the threat from 138 Brigade, many were shot down before the attack was called off.

At 2.20pm a German bombing party retaliated, attacking the barrier at the end of Big Willie. Sergeant Beard and a section of 'C' Company of the 1/5th South Staffordshire's managed to hold out until Lieutenant H Hakes arrived with reinforcements. This was just the beginning of the counterattacks. Sensing that the Staffordshire Brigade had suffered grievous casualties, the Germans struck:

A number of Germans in the SOUTH FACE trench got out of their trench and attempted to cross to BIG WILLIE but were driven back with loss by rapid fire from No 10 Platoon. The German bomb attack came over the second barrier into the space between the two barriers and was there engaged by our bombers who drove the enemy back again beyond the second barrier, 8696 Sergeant J Beard and 7952 Private W Barnes doing good work with the bayonet. At this point our men came under bomb fire from three directions, right, front and half left, and were forced to retire to the first barrier....

After a fierce struggle the Germans withdrew, leaving Brigadier-General Feetham's men to reorganise.

The Staffordshire Brigade's first battle had been an unmitigated disaster. Nearly one thousand officers and men had been killed or injured, the majority in the first ten minutes. Instead of capturing the Dump, the Brigade was left struggling to maintain its position in Big Willie Trench. The final words on the attack belong to an anonymous staff officer who eagerly watched the events unfold from the headquarters dugout:

It was wonderful seeing the great smoke cloud along the front, and then five minutes before the bombardment stopped, the figures crawling over the parapet and lying down in front, as far as you could see either side. At the moment the guns lifted, all got up and began to run or rather jog. Then they all seemed to melt away ....

46th Division's attack on Hohenzollern Redoubt. Fosse 8 is visible through the smoke. IWM - Q29001

138 (Lincolnshire and Leicestershire) Brigade's attack on Hohenzollen Redoubt

Brigadier-General Geoffrey Kemp planned to advance across the redoubt with two battalions, the 1/5th Lincolns on the left and 1/4th Leicesters to the right. Once the redoubt had fallen, bombing parties would fan out behind, working their way down Little Willie and Big Willie Trenches. While the assault troops continued towards Fosse Trench, additional bomb squads would follow, clearing North Face and South Face. The 1/4th Lincolns would follow in support, consolidating the Redoubt and provide bombing parties. On this occasion an emphasis had been placed on bringing equipment forward. All too often assault troops were forced to evacuate an area because they lacked sandbags and entrenching tools. The Divisional pioneer battalion, the 1/1st Monmouths, would follow the Staffordshire Brigade onto the Redoubt, loaded with supplies.

As zero hour approached, smoke candles and grenades were used to thicken the gas cloud. Precisely at 2.00am the first wave moved forward, crossing the front parapet of the Redoubt unmolested. The second wave followed and it seemed as though the Germans were unprepared. The third line was delayed moving through the narrow trenches, with a subsequent knock-on effect on the subsequent waves. The delay meant that the smoke was clearing by the time they started and the machine guns in Mad Point soon trained on their new target. The enfilading fire inflicted a heavy toll on any one who tried to cross No Man's Land.

The 1/1st Monmouths came next. They were intent on reaching the Chord, the trench that marked the north east limit of Hohenzollen Redoubt. With losses mounting they reached their objective, only to find it battered beyond recognition. The Chord resembled a shallow ditch, peppered with shell holes and incapable of sheltering anybody. Despite the early success the attack now faltered. The open ground in front of Fosse Trench was swept with cross-fire not only from Mad Point, but from South Face Trench. Two machine-guns taken by the retreating Germans began to inflict grievous casualties on the 1/5th Lincolns and the 1/4th Leicesters. Only one officer, Captain R E Madge of the 1/5th Leicesters, survived unscathed. Leaderless, the survivors began to fall back or seek shelter where they could.

Meanwhile, the bombing parties had failed to make any progress. Big Willie Trench had been filled in, and the squad was wiped out as it tried to bypass the blockage. The group detailed to enter Little Willie Trench lay either dead or wounded in No Man's Land, victims of Mad

Point's machine-guns. The Germans had managed to block North and South Face trenches before they fled. Corporal C Leadbeater took charge of the squad in North Face when his officer fell. In the ensuing bomb encounter (that continued throughout the night), his group managed to hold their own and barricaded the trench. Leadbeater was recommended for the Distinguished Conduct Medal, his second recommendation in a fortnight.

With his Brigade in danger of retiring from the Redoubt, Brigadier-General Kemp ordered B Company of the 1/5th Leicesters forward to support the attack. Lieutenant Wollaston, manning the machine-guns in the front line, had already made a single-handed attempt to rally the retiring troops. Climbing out into No Man's Land, he encouraged a few forward, but was knocked to the ground by a shell burst. In spite of a splinter wound, he gathered a small party of men and led them into Little Willie Trench. The group managed to clear eighty metres of trench before their ammunition ran out.

While Wollaston conducted his personal crusade, Captain Edward Langdale MC led B Company over the top. Although the small force drew fire from every direction, Langdale seemed unaffected by the death and destruction around him:

> *Walking along with his pipe in his mouth, Captain Langdale might have been at a field day, as he calmly signalled his right platoon to keep up in line, with 'Keep it up Oakham'.*

Many stragglers joined Langdale's company, but by the time they had crossed No Man's Land all five company officers had been hit.

Official History summary of 46th Division's disastrous attack.

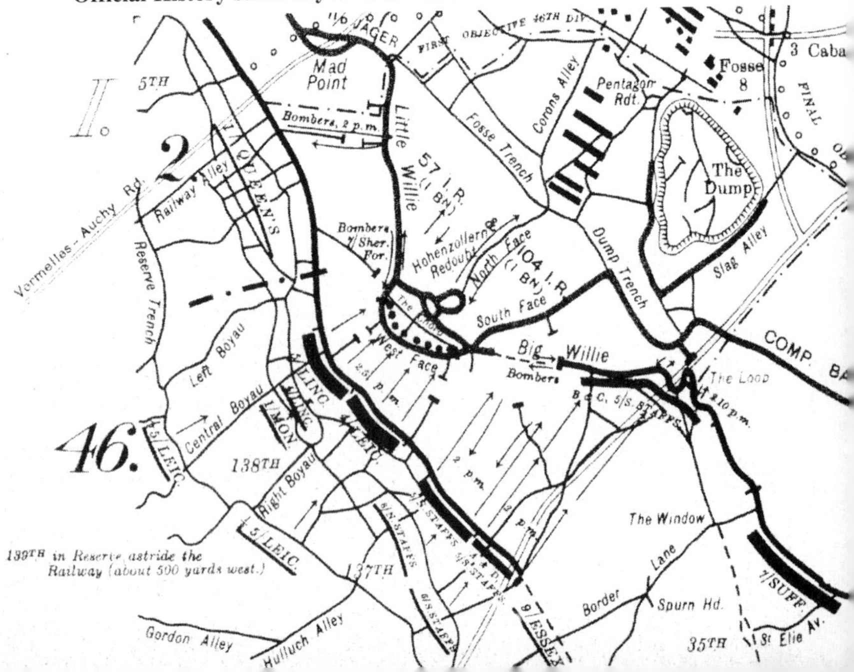

Captain Langdale was the last to fall, shot in the head near the German parapet. Without officers the company disintegrated and men found cover where they could on the Redoubt. A Company followed and a few entered West Face Trench, Captain Paulyn Rawdon-Hastings dying at the head of the bayonet charge. The only surviving officer, Second Lieutenant Tomson, decided to go no further, instructing his men to consolidate the trench.

By 3.30pm the attack was over. Isolated parties of the Lincolns and Leicesters were holding out in the West Face of the redoubt. Apart from the wounded and dying, the only men ahead of the Redoubt was Captain Madge's small group. As Battalion Machine-gun Officer, Madge had taken three gun teams forward. Only one gun remained, minus a tripod, and only two boxes of ammunition. Seeking cover in a battered trench Sergeant Drewery operated the gun while Madge directed his fire. The rest of his party braved the crossfire to collect ammunition boxes from the dead. Madge's party eventually returned after dusk, having kept the Germans at bay for over two hours. In Madge's own words:

> *We went into the show about twenty three officers and about eight hundred and fifty men and came out with one officer and one hundred and ten men .... Nothing could have been more admirable than the way the men behaved in this, their first battle.*

The Germans followed up and throughout the night attempted to retake West Face Trench. Second Lieutenant Tomson, of the 1/5th Leicester's, spent the night behind one of the barricades, throwing endless numbers of bombs to keep them at bay. He and his men

Medics wait for the wounded to arrive in Vermelles. IWM - Q29006

Captain Charles Vickers VC.

smoked continuously so that the fuses could be lit. When the rum ration arrived the following morning Tomson complained that he had eaten nothing *'but two biscuits and over 300 cigarettes'* since the attack began.

The following day the 139 (Sherwood Foresters) Brigade occupied the front line positions. In Little Willie Trench the 1/7th Sherwood's faced numerous bombing attacks and, as night approached, Captain Charles Vickers was instructed to relieve Captain Warren. The attacks continued after dark and Vickers' party lost heavily. Manning the barricade, he held back the Germans for several hours, aided by two men who kept him supplied with bombs. In the meantime Vickers ordered a second barrier to be built to his rear, leaving the three men isolated. Eventually, his luck ran out when a bomb destroyed the barrier, severely wounding him. His bravery had ensured that the Redoubt remained securely in British hands.

Captain Vickers received the Victoria Cross the following January. In the summer he returned to France for a six month period, before being recalled to England as an instructor. He returned for a third tour, seeing action throughout 1918, rising to the rank of acting major. During the Second World War Vickers worked in the Ministry of Economic Warfare. He went to work for a number of professional bodies, and published numerous papers and books. He was knighted for his services in the sailing world, participating in many competitions, including the Fastnet Race. Colonel Sir Charles Vickers died in 1982, aged 87.

46th Division's memorial

It was 46th Division's first, and one of its bloodiest, battles. The two assault brigades had suffered heavily, nearly three thousand casualties. The fact that a Divisional memorial was built on the outskirts of Vermelles, overlooking Hohenzollern Redoubt, is testament to the influence the battle had on those who survived.

Chapter Ten

12th (EASTERN) DIVISION

The plan for Major-General Arthur Scott's 12th (Eastern) Division had two objectives. First Army was anxious to secure Hulluch Quarries, to prevent the Germans from using it as a base to launch counter-attacks. To achieve this two attacks would converge on the Quarries; 35 Brigade attacking with two battalions from the west, while 37 Brigade advanced from the south with a single battalion. It was hoped that this approach would prevent the German machine-guns from concentrating in any one direction. The second part of the Divisional plan called for a single battalion to retake Gun Trench, depriving the Germans of their observation posts over the British rear. Although gas would take no part in discomforting the defence, a smoke screen, made by candles and smoke grenades, was planned to cover the advance.

35 Brigade's Attack

On the left, the 7th Suffolks planned to attack the north west corner of the quarry. While A and D companies bombed their way forward along two parallel communication trenches, B Company would cross No Man's Land. The 7th Norfolks planned a similar combined assault on the south west corner of the quarry. Their jumping off line formed a semi-circle, and the Germans held the trench in front known as the

Trench map covering Hulluch Quarries, the Hairpin projects towards the western corner of the Quarry.

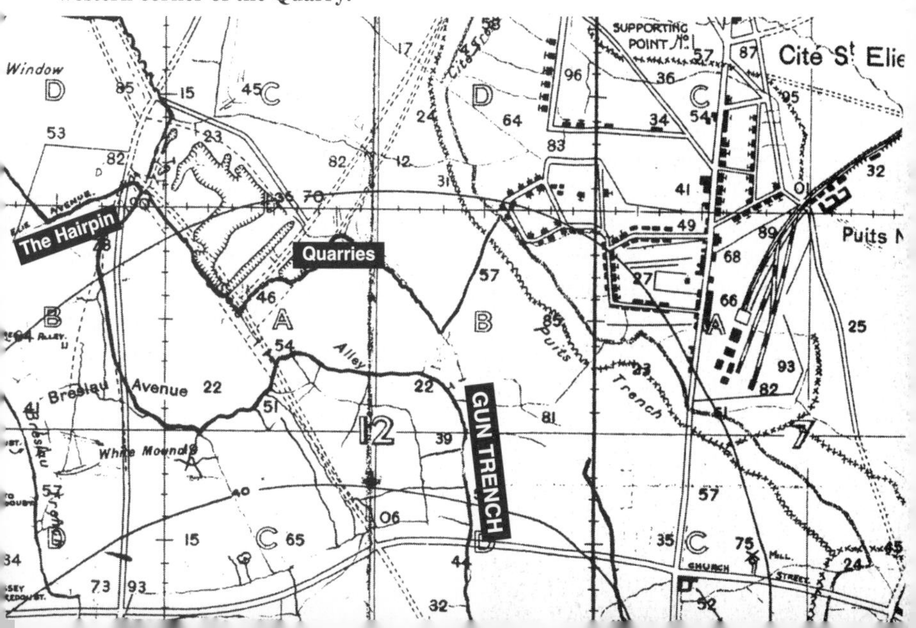

Gas release in progress prior to zero hour. IWM - Q29003

Chord. The Norfolks objective was to take the Chord and close the arc. The plan called for the Battalion bombers to work their way up two communication trenches on the left, west of the Quarries. Bombers from the 5th Royal Berkshires would lead B company on the right flank, with the intention of working their way round the east side of the Quarries. It was hoped that the two-pronged approach would encircle the garrison. Meanwhile, C and D Companies would advance over the top in a frontal attack on the Chord.

As zero hour approached a misunderstanding meant that the smoke-screen failed to achieve any purpose, the Norfolks' war diary complains that;

> *By some mistake the smoke cloud, which was being produced by the Guards, stopped at 1.40pm.*

Without a smoke screen to protect them, both battalions came under fire as soon as they left their trenches. The Brigade was exposed to crossfire from the Quarries and from Slag Alley to its left. The Suffolks also received attention from the German machine-guns on the Dump.

The attack across No Man's Land by Major Vere Currey's B Company was doomed without the assistance of the smoke screen. Half the company fell victim to the intense crossfire; Currey was killed at the outset. The survivors withdrew to their jumping off trench and eventually followed A Company along the communication trench.

The left hand bombing party of the Suffolks managed to rush the first barrier, although A Company's CO, Captain Charles Cobbold, died leading the charge. Pushing forward they made good progress and eventually reached the edge of the Quarries. Meanwhile D Company was experiencing difficulties breaking through the barrier barring their way. When Captain Henry fell wounded, Captain Charles Sorley took over leading the bombers forward in a reckless charge. Sorley was killed at the barricade, but his sacrifice had opened the way forward for

D Company. With the obstacle cleared, Lieutenant Deighton led the survivors (D Company suffered 160 casualties in the attack) forward along the communications trench. Deighton eventually linked up with A Company at the north west corner of the quarry, closing what was known as The Hairpin. Both Captain Chitty-Thomas and Lieutenant Deighton received the Military Cross for their leadership.

Charles Sorley.

Captain Charles Sorley was born in Aberdeen in 1895. His parents moved to Cambridge five years later and Charles was educated at Marlborough College. Although he obtained a scholarship for University College, Oxford, he never attended. In the summer of 1914, Sorley was arrested whilst on holiday in the Moselle valley. He was quickly released and ordered to leave Germany. On his return Sorley was commissioned and joined the 7th Suffolks. The following March the Battalion left for France, spending time holding trenches in Ploegsteert Wood, south of Ypres. Shortly after he arrived in France it was suggested that he should print a slim volume of his verse. He declined:

> *Besides, this is no time for oliveyards and vineyards, more especially of the small-holdings type. For three years or the duration of the war, let be.*

After his death a number of his poems were published in *Marlborough and Other Poems* and *The Poems and Selected Letters of Charles Hamilton Sorley.* He is remembered as one of the war poets. Charles Sorley's body was never recovered and his name is carved on the panels of the Loos Memorial to the Missing.

As zero hour approached, observers on the 7th Norfolks' front could see the Germans moving into position in their fire trench. The assistance hoped for from trench mortars, in the destruction of machine-gun posts and trench blocks, failed to materialise:

> *The mortar should have demolished the barricades for bombers left and right. This was not successfully carried out and owing to this one squad was wiped out getting through.*

The squad mentioned belonged to the Berkshires on the right flank. The machine-gun positioned behind the barricade could not be dislodged and many died, including Captain Philip Preston, in their efforts to silence the gun. Lieutenant Franklin's team also struggled to make progress on the left. They suffered many casualties, clearing only fifty metres of trench.

The attack in the centre by C and D companies was also doomed to fail. As soon as the men emerged from their trench they came under close range enfilade fire from the south end of the Quarry. Fifty men eventually reached the objective and managed to clear two hundred yards of the Chord. They were, however, isolated and, with both bombing teams checked, the only way to support them was over the top. Lieutenant-Colonel F E Walter ordered A Company and six platoons of the Royal Berkshires forward to help consolidate the captured trench. They were mown down within twenty yards, leaving C and D companies to fend off counter-attacks alone. With no hope of reinforcements, they were forced to withdraw when their bombs ran out. Altogether the 7th Norfolks suffered 430 casualties.

37 Brigade's attack

The right hand brigade of the 12th Division, led by Brigadier-General Charles Fowler, had two separate objectives. The 6th Buffs were to attack north and capture the section of Gun Trench projecting east from the Quarries. The plan was to link up 35 Brigade and complete a protective flank to the quarry. Meanwhile, the 7th East Surreys would secure the last remaining section of Gun Trench in German hands. A successful attack by both battalions would give XI Corps a continuous front facing Cité St Elie and Hulluch.

The Buffs were faced with an advance across open ground, and in this sector No Man's Land was over 300 metres wide. The Germans had only just finished the trench to be attacked, and its exact position was as yet unknown. Consequently the artillery barrage, effectively firing blind, failed to damage the German position. Of the attack itself there is little to tell. Although smoke candles were used, the wind was insufficient to carry the screen far. Against a well-prepared enemy, the Buffs stood no chance; the machine-gun fire was so effective that no one advanced more than one hundred metres. Nine officers and over four hundred men were killed or wounded.

The 7th East Surreys were more successful, employing combined 'rush and bomb' tactics. At 2.00pm two platoons of 'B' Company, led by Lieutenant Watts, charged across No Man's Land. Its appears that the Germans were surprised, for Gun Trench was taken without difficulty and many Germans fled. 'A' Company was not so fortunate. By the time that Captain Vigor Tomkins men moved out into the open, a machine-gun was waiting for them. The two lines of men were shot to pieces, and the senior surviving NCO, Sergeant Martin, was forced

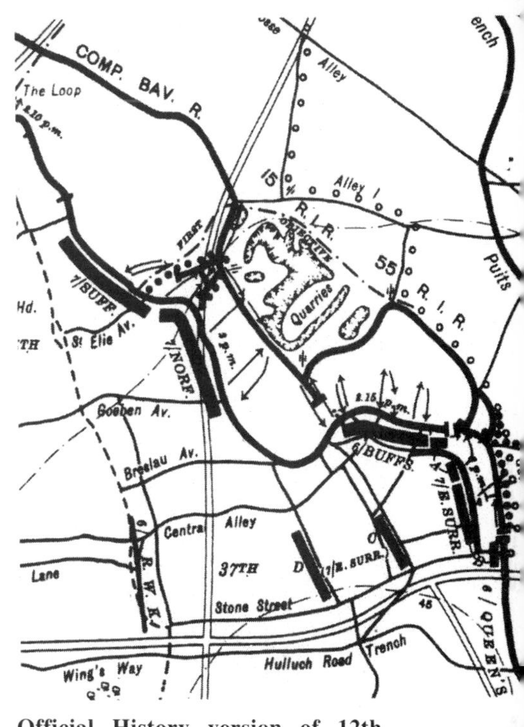

Official History version of 12th Division's attack on 13 October.

to withdrawn the survivors to Central Alley.

In the meantime Lieutenant Findlay's bomb squads had made good progress and they had been able to link up with B Company in Gun Trench. The Buffs then set about building barricades in the maze of trenches, blocking all those leading towards the German lines. With the objective firmly in the East Surreys hands, Lieutenant-Colonel R Baldwin sent his final two companies forward to complete the consolidation work. It had been one of the few successes of the day.

As darkness fell across the battlefield, General Haig had to resign himself to the fact that the Hohenzollern Redoubt would stay in German hands for the winter. Bad weather and a lack of resources meant that there could be no more attacks. First Army planners would have to find another way to capture the Redoubt.

Wounded arriving in Vermelles in search of assistance. IWM - Q29005

Chapter Eleven

MINING HOHENZOLLERN REDOUBT

Within days of the battle ending, a new tunnelling company arrived on I Corps front. Captain Frank Preedy and 170th Tunnelling Company RE were charged with the task of mining Hohenzollern Redoubt. Digging down through the clay they were horrified to find that Germans miners were already active beneath the British trenches. Mines were immediately laid and detonated, destroying both British and German tunnels. Captain Preedy proposed to drive the Germans back by digging a series of tunnels, twenty metres apart. As soon as his men heard the Germans they would detonate small mine. These mines, known as camouflets, were designed to destroy tunnels while leaving the surface intact. Having blown a mine, adjacent tunnels were driven forward, converging inwards towards repair works. The work was dangerous and nerve-wracking, but the tactic proved successful. Three months, and over fifty mines later, Preedy's men were under the Redoubt. While the tunnellers fought an underground war at a shallow level, three deeper tunnels were being pushed forward with the aid of drills. By February 1916 the three charges had been set, totalling over twenty-five tonnes of ammonal.

A mine detonates under a German trench.

Major-General Scott's 12th (Eastern) Division moved into the sector at the end of the month and two battalions of 37 Brigade were chosen to capture the craters. The left of 8th Royal Fusiliers had to secure two of the proposed craters (B and C) along with an existing crater. Meanwhile, the right of the battalion would secure the northern section of the Chord. The 9th Royal Fusiliers faced the right half of Hohenzollern, they would occupy the rest of the Chord and the third new crater (A). Both battalions expected to find more craters on their front.

At 5.45pm on the 2 March the Redoubt erupted throwing tons of earth, men and materials into the air. George

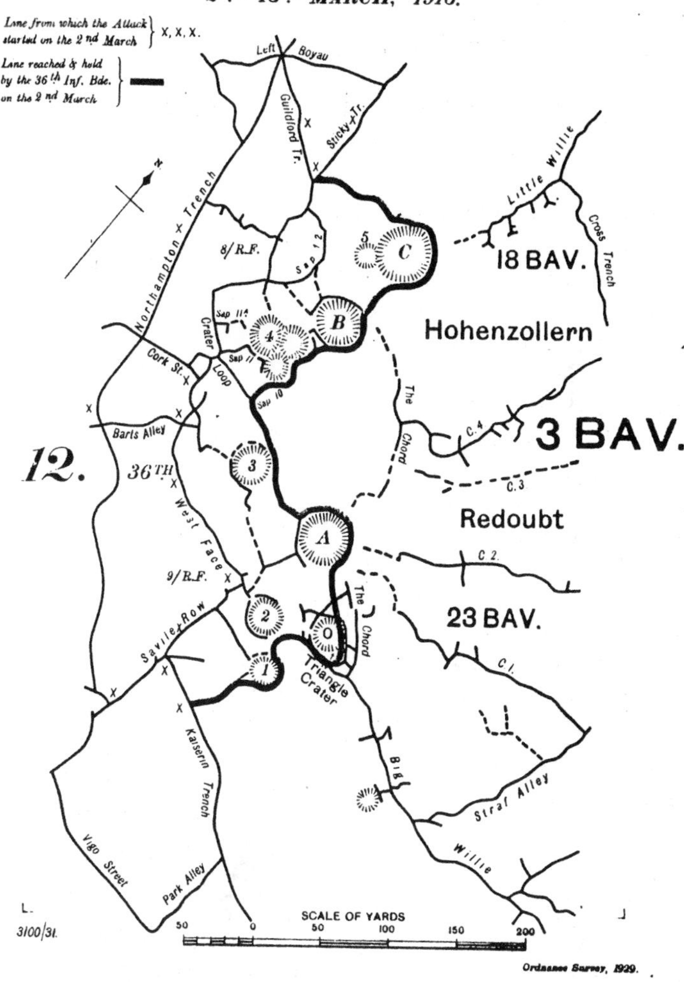

Coppard witnessed a mine detonating and the description in his autobiography, *With a Machine Gun to Cambrai,* is particularly graphic:

> *At the moment of explosion the ground trembled violently in a miniature earthquake. Then, like an enormous pie-crust rising up, slowly at first, the bulging mass of earth cracked in thousands of fissures. When the vast sticky mass could no longer contain the pressure beneath, the centre burst open, and the energy released carried all before it. Hundreds of tons of earth were hurled skywards to a height of three hundred feet or more, many of the lumps of great size.*

Exhausted troops consolidate a mine crater.

Parties under Captain Chard, Lieutenant Upward and Company-Sergeant-Major Sharp successfully secured all three craters on the left of the 8th Royal Fusiliers. Debris from the mine showered the right section and many were buried. Machine-gun fire made short work of the survivors as they advanced, killing or wounding all but two men. Captain Mason, leading the support section, found the Chord to be non-existent and was forced to seek cover in the necklace of craters marking the perimeter of the redoubt. With the aid of reinforcements, brought up by Major Cope, the 8th Fusiliers were able to dig in.

The 9th Fusiliers were also affected by the detonations. Fifty men of B Company, under Captain the Honourable R Phillips, were waiting in the fire trench when the mines exploded. Half were temporarily put out of action, buried under falling debris. Despite the setback, the rest of Phillips' party secured the right section of the Chord. C Company, under Captain Elliot Cooper, captured the third crater along with three old craters. Sergeant Cromyn then led a party of bombers into Big Willie Trench. After making some progress they were forced to retire, having exhausted their supply of bombs.

With the craters secured, Captain Preedy's men came forward to search for tunnels. The main entrance was found in Triangle Crater and a nerve-wracking exploration followed. Preparations were started to dismantle the tunnels but before they were complete, the Germans reacted.

On the afternoon of 4 March a strong counter-attack rushed Triangle Crater, recapturing the entrance to the tunnel complex. Two

Aerial photograph of Fosse 8. The Dump is top right and the craters on Hohenzollern Redoubt are bottom right. IWM - Q44167

days later C Company of the 6th Buffs retaliated. Corporal William Cotter's party became bogged down in deep mud as it tried to reach Triangle Crater. Faced with machine-guns and showered with bombs from the lip of the crater, the Buffs fell back to No 2 Crater. Corporal Cotter was severely wounded, losing part of his right leg, as well as injuries to his arms. Even so he remained in command, issuing orders and directing fire against counterattacks that lasted for nearly two hours. Only then did Cotter allow his wounds to be dressed, although it was another fourteen hours before he could be evacuated. He died two days later at Lillers Casualty Clearing Station and his grave is situated in the Communal Cemetery. For his part in saving the Buffs' positions, Corporal Cotter was posthumously awarded the Victoria Cross.

Inside the Hohenzollern Redoubt.

With the tunnels in German hands there were concerns that the Redoubt could erupt at any moment. To counter the danger, 170th Tunnelling Company burrowed into the German mining system and, finding them empty, began preparing them for demolition. On 12 March a series of explosions completely destroyed the system of galleries.

As the weather worsened the Germans resorted to shelling the craters with their *minenwerfer*, a devastating weapon that caused havoc in the craters. In the meantime they began new tunnels under the British line. At 5pm on the 18th the Redoubt erupted for a second time. On the right, the party of 7th East Surreys holding 'C' Crater, disappeared in the explosion. Only Company-Sergeant-Major Palmer and three others survived. The Germans followed up, driving Palmer's small group out of the crater field. A counterattack by Captain Scott eventually retook Crater No 4, leaving Craters B and C in German hands.

A second mine showered the three craters held by the 6th Buffs, blocking the communications trenches. None of the Buffs survived the blast and the Germans occupied them unopposed. Although it was some time before the 6th Royal West Kent were able to respond, their counterattack reached the nearest sides of the craters. No Man's Land now consisted of a necklace of interlocking craters, a morass that neither side could cross.

Nightfall brought a close to the intense fighting on the Redoubt. The 12th Division had suffered 3,000 casualties during the two weeks of fighting, a large number considering the small area of ground fought over.

Chapter Twelve

TOURING I CORPS AREA

The car tour is designed to give the visitor an introduction to I Corps area. The route is almost six miles long, completing a circuit of the battlefield. Drivers need to be aware that many of the roads can be fast and busy, particularly during peak periods. A great deal of commercial traffic passes through the area on weekdays. Drivers are strongly advised to concentrate on the road rather than taking in the view. There are times along the route when it is possible to park a vehicle safely, but on the main roads it would be considered an offence, as well as extremely dangerous, to obstruct the other road users.

The sketch map shows the main landmarks and points of interest. This does have advantages as well as drawbacks and it may be wise to study the route on a road map first. Although industry has overrun parts of the battlefield, particularly around the Brickstacks and Cité St Elie, the majority of the area has not altered. There are a number of landmarks that become familiar after a while, in particular the slagheap that stands close to Hulluch Quarries near Cité St Elie.

Starting Point - Vermelles Church

Vermelles is well sign posted off the N43, the main route between Bethune and Lens. From either town, the conical peak of the slagheap at Philosophe gives adequate warning that it is time to slow down ready to turn into the village. There are two roads connecting Vermelles with the N43 and they both lead to

Car tour of I Corps area.

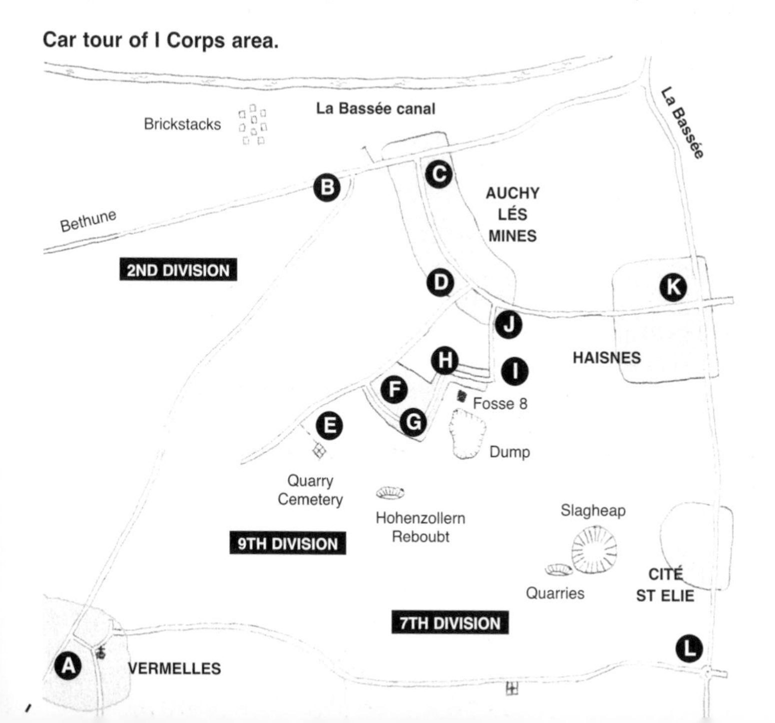

View north across 2nd Division's front, mine craters once filled this field. The Brickstacks were beyond the line of trees.

the centre of the village. If you miss one, be ready to take the second option. There are a number of small shops in the village, the first of a number of opportunities to buy provisions. The majority of shops in the area close at noon for an hour and a half and on certain days they close for the entire afternoon. So stock up early rather than go hungry later on!

With your back to the church, which served as an observation post for artillery observers, head north west along the main street. After 200m turn right at the T junction **(A)** onto the D75, sign posted for Auchy-lès-Mines and La Bassée. Before long the houses come to an end and fields line either side of the road. There is a large isolated house with dog kennels to the right of the road, 1/2 mile from the edge of the village. It was behind 2nd Division's front line during the battle and was used as a forward aid post, No Man's Land crossed the road 1/2 mile further on. On the 25th, 19 Brigade advanced to the east of the road, meeting heavy opposition; no one managed to reach the German trenches. The front line ran north across the fields to the line of poplar trees on the horizon. By September 1915 the area was cluttered with mine craters and the road crosses No Man's Land at Mine Point. Only a handful of 6 Brigade's men managed to enter the German fire trench. The poplar trees mentioned screen the Brickstacks from view, the stacks disappeared many years ago during the construction of an electricity substation. The La Bassée Canal and 5 Brigade area are beyond the Brickstacks.

Continue to the T junction at the end of the road **(B)**, turning right onto the N41 heading for La Bassée. Enter Auchy-lès-Mines and after 1/2 mile turn right at the traffic lights sign into the centre of the village **(C)**. The CWGC sign for Quarry Cemetery is partially obscured by directional signs. There is a good selection of shops lining the high street, providing most items you would need for a day on the battlefield. After 1/2 mile turn right at the CWGC sign for Quarry Cemetery **(D)**, there is a local sign for Cité du 8. Heading out of the village there is a 1920s style housing estate, Cité du Madagascar, on the left after 1/2 mile. It was built to house the employees of Fosse 8 colliery once the mine resumed production. The last house on the left stands on the site of Mad Point, the

9th Division's front between Mad Point and Hohenzollern Redoubt.

machine gun post that decimated 28 Brigade of the 9th (Scottish) Division. The parking place for Quarry Cemetery, where you need to turn your car round, is 300 metres further on **(E)**.

Looking back to Mad Point it is possible to see the Scots view of the German positions. To the right a huge clump of bushes and trees marks the site of Hohenzollern Redoubt. A number of electricity pylons help to indentify the locality. Little Willie Trench, where three acts of bravery resulted in the award of the Victoria Cross, ran between the Redoubt and Mad Point. Retracing your steps past Mad Point, take the first right into the estate **(F)**. Following the road to the end, turn left in front of the farm heading north through the estate **(G)**. After passing a sports centre on the right take the second right **(H)**, Boulevard de la Fosse, opposite Relax Bar. Following the road, note that Corons Trench, the perimeter held first by the Scots and then 73 Brigade, ran to the rear of the houses on the left. Fosse 8 winding tower, now an overgrown mound of rubble, stood behind the wall on the right towards the end of the road. Two large houses and Tip-Top Bar stand around the junction at the end, known as Trois Cabarets in 1915. The inexperienced men of 73 Brigade held onto the junction for three days before the Germans struck.

Turn left at the junction **(I)**, heading north towards Auchy. Leaving Trois Cabarets, it is possible to see Haisnes on the horizon to the right. On a clear day the church tower can be seen. The open slope leading up to the village and the German Second Line became a death trap once German reserves had arrived. Taking up positions either side of the water tower in front, they were able to stop any reinforcements reaching Haisnes. Continue north passing Auchy-lèz-Mines cemetery on the left. A German Jagër Battalion took up positions in the cemetery on the morning of the 25th, preventing 26 Brigade from advancing beyond Fosse 8. At the T Junction **(J)**, turn right for Haisnes.

View from Trois Cabarets looking towards Haisnes and Pekin Trench.

Passing the water tower to your left, continue into Haisnes. After a mile there is a main crossroads **(K)**, turn right heading for Lens. For a time Haisnes was wide open for capture; however, the Scots were delayed moving through the assembly trenches. By the time they arrived, three hours after zero, German reserves had moved forward from La Bassée, barring the way. Heading south through Cité St Elie take note of the slagheap to the right, it stands close to the Hulluch Quarries. Just beyond Cité St Elie, take a right turn at the mini roundabout **(L)**. On the morning of the 25th elements of 20 Brigade reached this point, known as Estaminet Corner in 1915. As the Gordon Highlanders took up positions they were shocked to see a battalion of men, with a mounted officer at its head, entering Cité St Elie. The Highlanders opened fire as soon as the Germans turned onto the main road, scattering them. The Germans went on to occupy the defences covering Cité St Elie, containing 7th Division's attacks throughout the day.

Having taken the turning at the crossroads, head west back onto the battlefield. On the morning of the 25th, 20th Brigade advanced parallel road, capturing a number of artillery pieces dug in north of the road. St Mary's ADS Cemetery appears on the left, a mile from the crossroads. It stands in the centre of No Man's Land, 7th Division advanced across the fields to the right. Gas hampered many of the assault troops as they made their way across to the German trenches 400m away. The wind failed to carry the gas far enough and the German machine guns caused hundreds of casualties as the men cut through the broken wire. Hulluch Quarries, scene of bitter fighting towards the end of the battle, lies hidden behind the trees at the foot of the slagheap.

On a clear day it is possible to see Hohenzollen Redoubt, crowned with trees and electricity pylons on the horizon to the north west. Continuing east, take the opportunity for a brief look across IV Corps area to the left. The memorial to the men of the 46th Division who lost their lives on Hohenzollern Redoubt is a mile past the cemetery, on the outskirts of Vermelles. Carry on into the centre of Vermelles to your starting point at the church.

Having taken a brief tour around the battlefield, you can now decide which walks to follow. The circuit to reach the starting points follows, with a couple of minor detours, the same route as the car tour.

Looking north from the Hulluch - Vermelles road across No Man's Land on 7th Division's front.

HOHENZOLLERN

FOSSE 8

WALKING TOURS OF I CORPS BATTLEFIELD

Walking Tour 1 - 6 and 19 Brigades

From Vermelles take the D75, heading for Auchy-lès-Mines. Half a mile beyond the edge of the village there is a white farmhouse, with attached dog kennels, to your right. Five hundred metres beyond, where the road swings slightly to the right, pull in where a tractor trail heads across the fields to the left **(1)**. Although the verge looks wide there is only space for one car; ditches lurk in the grass either side of the pull in.

The church towers in the area are useful for orientation. To the west is the white tower of Cambrin Church; Cuinchy Church, near the canal, is to the north west. Looking north east, Auchy church can be seen through the trees. Following the tractor trail across the fields, the support trenches of 19 Brigade were to the right, Kingsway Trench ran along the eastern side of the track.

Mining activities had turned No Man's Land in this area into a quagmire. Craters, with rims of earth two or three metres high, blocked the way forward. The two lines were so close that the Germans held one lip of the craters while

Walking Tour 1 - 6 and 19 Brigades, south of the La Bassée Canal.

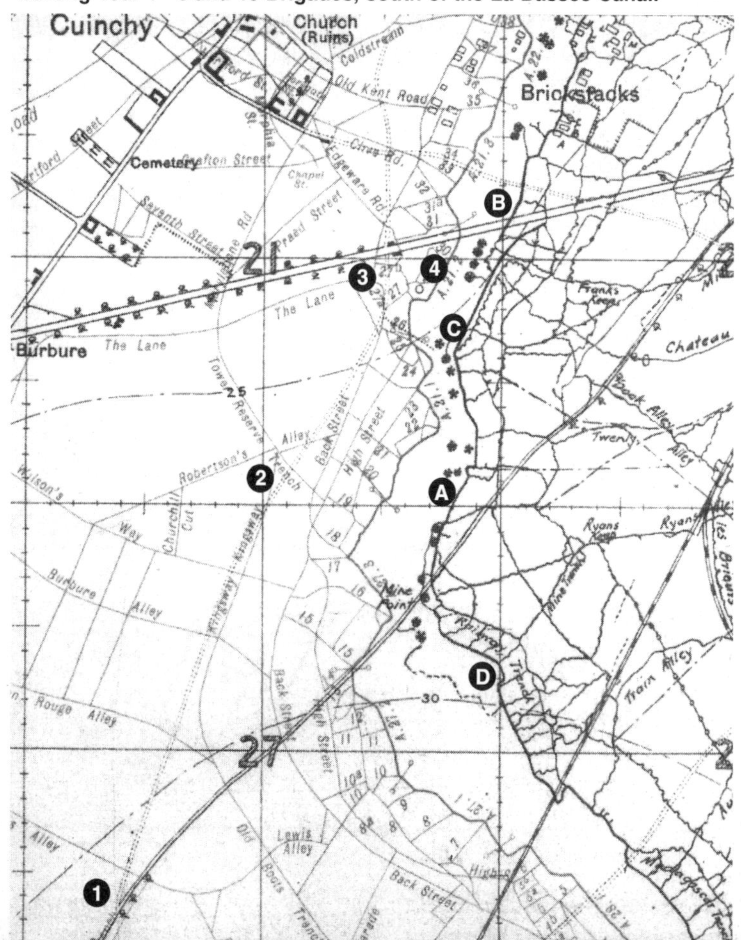

Looking east from 19 Brigade's trenches, Auchy church is visible on the horizon.

the British held the opposite side. Where No Man's Land crossed the Vermelles road, shown as Mine Point on British maps, the ground was fiercely contested. The 2nd Argyll and Sutherland Highlanders were forced to attack on a narrow front through a gap between the craters. Only a handful of men of the two leading platoons made it across to Mine Trench **(A)**; the support companies were decimated before they crossed the fire trench.

About 900 metres from the road, a second tractor trail forks to the left **(2)**, heading towards a water tower. The British front trench in this area was known as The Parade. With your back to the tower take time to view the battlefield, Auchy Church (19 Brigade's main objective), can be seen on the horizon to the east.

French Memorial to the men that died during the first winter of the war.

Continue along the track until a main road, the Bethune - La Bassée road, is reached **(3)**. To the right, fifty metres away, is a grey obelisk **(4)**, standing on raised ground. Cut through what once must have been a fine avenue of bushes to the French memorial. It remembers the men of the 58th (Territorial) Division who held this sector prior to the British. The Division arrived in the area on 14 October 1914, they were transferred to this sector from the Vosges region during the so-called Race for the Sea. Until May 1915 they faced the German 29th Division. The sad irony is that many of those holding the trenches opposite the French were from Alsace and Lorraine, the lost provinces of the 1870-71 war, handed back to France after the Great War.

The memorial stands on the British front line, near the junction of 6 Brigade and 19 Brigade. Looking north, across the road, the front line ran to the western tip of the line of poplar trees. The infamous Brickstacks, where the 1st Staffords attacked, lay beyond the trees, on the southern bank of the La Bassée canal. The brickfields disappeared many years ago during the construction of an electricity sub-station; this in turn has since been abandoned.

Looking south from the memorial across No Man's Land, across the site of Vesuvius and Etna craters.

On the morning of 25 September the 1st King's advanced astride the road towards Brickstacks Trench **(B)**. The company south of the road was annihilated crossing No Man's Land. Meanwhile, B Company became disorientated by the smoke and veered south across the road. They too met fierce opposition, becoming pinned down in front of uncut wire. Lieutenant James Ryan, the acting company commander, ran back down the road to notify Lieutenant-Colonel Potter of the disaster. He subsequently returned to his men and was never seen again. His actions saved the remaining companies of the King's from a similar fate.

Immediately south of the memorial is a sunken area. Just beyond it two large craters, known as Vesuvius and Etna, filled No Man's Land **(C)**.

The fighting died down in this sector while the battle raged on further south. On 27 September 1915 the 1/1st Hertfordshires was supposed to carry out a further attack on Brickstacks Trench, in the hope of drawing attention away from Fosse 8. Gas was employed but, for a second time, the wind failed to carry it far enough. Patrols sent out to test the German reactions were met by heavy fire. Major-General Horne wisely called off the action, but before the Hertfordshires could disperse disaster struck. A minenwerfer shell landed in one of the crowded bays, failing to explode. Private Alfred Burt ran over to the bomb and by bracing his foot against the casing, managed to pull out the fuse. By defusing the shell Burt saved many lives, his selfless act of bravery was rewarded with the Victoria Cross. Burt survived the war, rising to the rank of sergeant. He died in Watford in 1962, aged 67.

Corporal Arthur Burt VC

Three weeks later the men of 2nd King's Own were in the Brickstacks, recovering from their ordeals on Hohenzollern Redoubt. Minenwerfers played havoc with the Battalion's front line, which incorporated a number of interlocking craters. On 18 October mortar shells forced the evacuation of one of the craters, and in the confusion three men were found to be missing. Private Harry Christian braved the shells to return, finding his friends buried under debris. One at a time, he dug the men out, carrying them back to safety. Afterwards

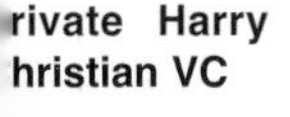

rivate Harry hristian VC

Christian sought out an exposed vantage point, so that he could warn his comrades of incoming shells. Christian received the Victoria Cross for saving many lives. He survived the war, despite contracting malaria in Salonika; he died in 1963, aged 82.

Return to where your vehicle is parked. However, before moving on, cross the road (taking care of the fast moving traffic) to observe the fields beyond. The direction of the advance was again directed on Auchy Church. The trenches of the 1st Middlesex ran across the field about 400 metres away. Their attack came to a bloody standstill in front of Railway Trench **(D)**. The 2nd Royal Welch Fusiliers waited in the support trenches, near where you are standing. Private Frank Richards captures the tension and chaos in his autobiography Old Soldiers Never Die:

> Dawn broke at last and we were anxiously waiting for the time when the 'Grand Slam' commenced. The assembly trenches were about seven hundred yards behind our front line. Dann and I were closely watching to see our gas going over, which we were told would kill every German for over a mile in front of us and which none of us believed in. Our artillery were still sending them over and also the enemy's artillery had opened out and some of the shells were falling around our front line. At last we saw the gas going over in two or three places: it looked like small clouds rolling along close to the ground. The white clouds hadn't gone very far before they seemed to stop and melt away. I found out later that the wind that should have taken it across No Man's Land hadn't put in an appearance and the gas had spread back into our trenches. Shortly after machine-gun fire and rifle fire rung out and we guessed that the Argylls and the Middlesex had gone over without waiting for our intense bombardment.

The white house on the road south of your position was a dressing station, with dugouts for only twenty four stretcher cases. Guys Alley, the main communication trench in the area, had been dug sufficiently wide for wheeled stretchers. It was soon blocked with wounded and gassed men in search of medical attention.

Walking Tour 2 - 5 Brigade

Drive north, turning right at the end onto the N41, (the La Bassée road). Head into the outskirts of Auchy, and half a mile beyond the derelict electricity substation, turn left, sign-posted for Violaines. The road runs along the top of a raised embankment, before swinging right under a railway bridge. Immediately after crossing the canal, park in the pull in area to the left, by a farmhouse **(1)**. After taking a look down the canal towards Cuinchy Lock (which was behind the British lines), follow the narrow path heading west along the top of the embankment. Take note of the steep bank, to assess whether you can climb back up it later. After a short distance the path detours around a low mound covered in trees and undergrowth. This is the start of a huge spoil bank, created during the excavation of the canal. Following the path around the base of the mound, continue to head west; the open fields to the right were just behind the

German lines **(2)**.

The spoil bank has been enlarged in post war years. No Man's Land cut across the canal about four hundred metres from the start of the mound. The German front line ran from left to right and Givenchy, across the fields, stood behind the British line. In 1915 the Germans had fortified the end of the spoil bank, making use of its height advantage to dominate the British trenches. This was the site of Tortoise Redoubt **(A)** and the 9th Highland Light Infantry held the trenches opposite. The rest of 5 Brigade advanced across the fields to your right, capturing the German front line trench. They were cut down as they tried to advance to the support line. A mine was detonated just to the east of Givenchy, at the Duck's Bill **(B)**.

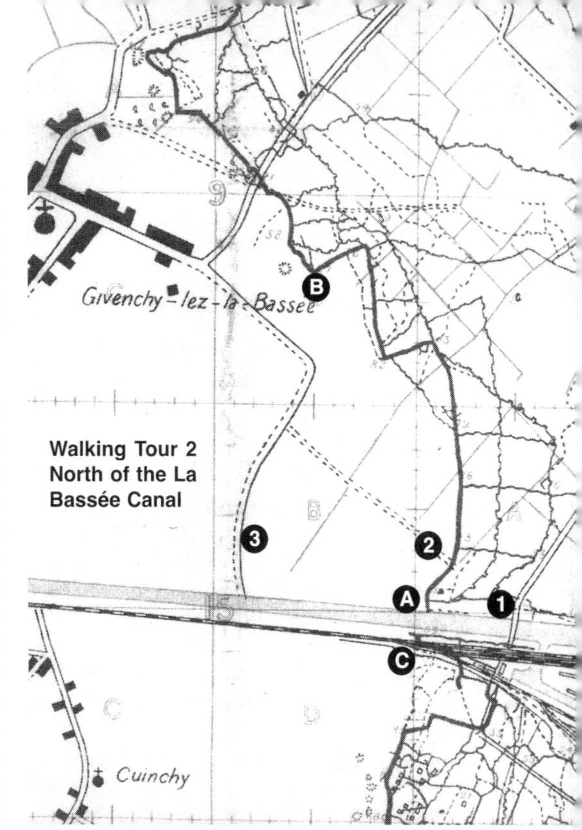

Walking Tour 2 North of the La Bassée Canal

The fields north of Tortoise Redoubt, scene of 5 Brigade's attack.

Looking west along the La Bassée Canal towards Cuinchy Lock. Captain Kilby VC was killed on the opposite bank, near the gap in the trees.

Carrying on towards Givenchy, the spoil heap ends abruptly. Turning left, follow the path down to the canal **(3)**. The embankment for the La Bassée - Bethune railway is on the opposite bank. German machine guns dug into the sides of the raised bank, at Embankment Redoubt **(C)**, were able to sweep both sides of the canal. On 1 February 1915 the Germans advanced along the embankment, capturing an advanced post of the 1st Irish Guards. Lance Corporal Michael O'Leary counter-attacked alone, seizing two enemy barricades. He went on to capture two machine gun posts, killing eight and capturing two crew men. He was awarded the Victoria Cross soon afterwards and was taken back to Ireland where he was treated as a national hero.

Lance-Corpora Michael O'Leary VC

On the morning of 25 September, C Company of the 1st South Staffordshires advanced along the towpath towards Embankment Redoubt. Drifting gas had incapacitated many before zero hour. However, Captain Kilby managed to rally the rest forward. Kilby was seriously wounded at the head of his men, losing a foot near the German wire. Despite the pain he urged his men forward, firing his rifle in encouragement. Even so, the attack failed and C Company were forced to withdraw, leaving their leader behind. A search party failed to recover Kilby's body that night, but the following month an observer spotted a white cross in No Man's Land. The inscription read:

> For King and Fatherland. In memory of Lieut. King and Lieut. Hall and eight men of the South Staffordshire Regiment who died like heroes.

Captain Arthur Kilby was posthumously awarded the Victoria Cross for leadership and bravery. His body was finally recovered in February 1929 and re-interred many miles away in Arras Road Cemetery at Roclincourt. Lieutenant Bruce Hall had managed to lead a small group of men into the German trenches south of the railway. They were overwhelmed and Hall's body was never found. His name appears on the Loos Memorial to the Missing at Dud Corner.

There are now two options to return to your vehicle. If you are able to climb the steep bank noted at the beginning, follow the canal path west towards the road bridge. Alternatively retrace your steps along the foot of the spoil bank.

Walking Tour 3 - Mad Point and Railway Redoubt

Returning to the N41 La Bassée road, turn left into the town. After half a mile turn right at the traffic lights, sign-posted for Auchy centre (Centré Ville). There is a CWGC sign for Quarry Cemetery at the junction, but it is partially hidden by direction signs. Head along the main street of the town, (where you may wish to purchase provisions for later), turn right at the Quarry Cemetery sign; the French road sign is marked Cité du 8. Just beyond the edge of the village, there is a pull in to your left provided for visitors to Quarry Cemetery **(1)**.

Before visiting the cemetery, walk south for about 200 metres where there are railway lines embedded in the tarmac **(2)**. The Vermelles railway, built to transport coal, ran to the north and south. The crossing provides an excellent viewpoint for most of I Corps battlefield. On a clear day it is possible to see the twin slag heaps that mark the southern extremity of First Army's attack. The modern estate of Cité Madagascar to the northeast stands to the left of Fosse 8 colliery. Hohenzollern Redoubt, the highest piece of ground in the immediate area, is marked by a large clump of trees, to the right of the estate. The slagheap to the east (which did not exist in 1915), masks Cité St Elie from view. Hulluch Quarries stood at the foot of the slagheap. 7th Division occupied the

Railway Redoubt, Mad Point and Quarry Cemetery.

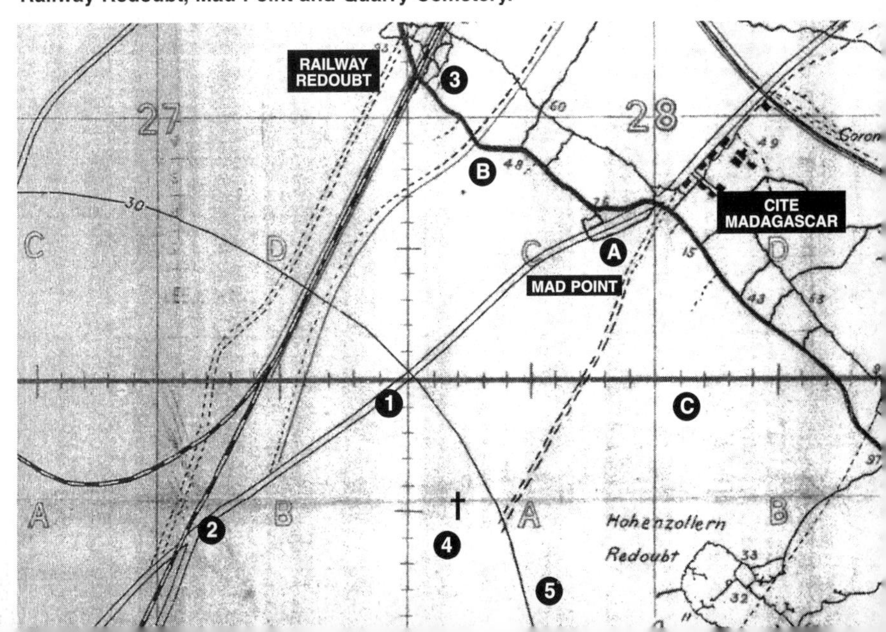

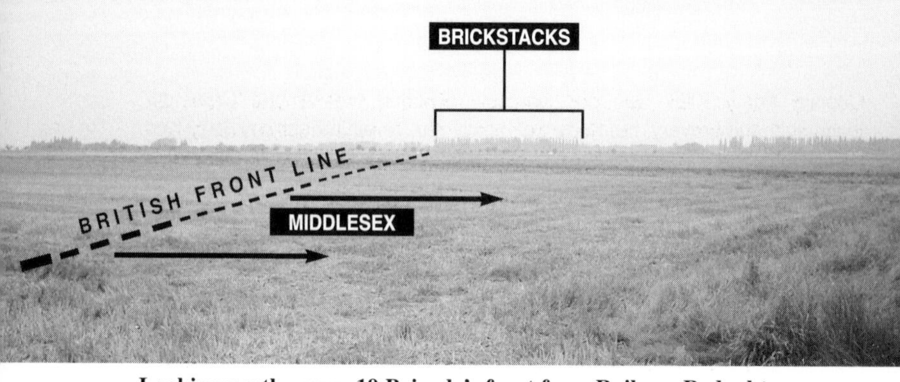

Looking north across 19 Brigade's front from Railway Redoubt.

open fields to the right. It is just possible to make out a Cross of Sacrifice, flanked by two clumps of trees, on the Hulluch road, close to the horizon. This is St Mary's ADS Cemetery, which stands in No Man's Land at the southern extremity of I Corps front.

On 25 September the railway marked the boundary between 2nd Division and 9th (Scottish) Division. Head north along the old railway line (now a purpose built footpath), to visit the site of Railway Redoubt. The 1st Middlesex held the ground to the left of the track, beyond the hawthorn bushes. At intervals it is possible to step between the bushes to obtain a view of 19 Brigade's sector. 2nd Division's front ran at an oblique angle to the railway. The poplar trees, on the horizon to the north, stand close to the site of the Brickstacks.

To the right a single house stands alongside the Auchy road **(A)**. This was the site of Mad Point, the German machine gun post that dominated the attacks in this area. In 1915 it jutted forward from the German front line, with gun slits positioned to enfilade any attacks. Mad Point house can be seen from most locations and is a useful orientation point for this part of the battlefield.

The 10th Highland Light Infantry advanced across the field to the right, between the railway and road. They never reached Madagascar Trench **(B)**, due to the crossfire directed from Mad Point and Railway Redoubt. The 6th Kings Own Scottish Borderers advanced beyond the road heading for the area covered by the housing estate. Little Willie Trench ran from left to right between Mad Point and Hohenzollern Redoubt. The position of the Redoubt is hidden beneath the bushes and trees, to the right of the estate, which are crowned by a double-headed electricity pylon.

The path rises slowly onto a shallow embankment about 800 metres from

Railway Redoubt's view of No Man's Land on 28 Brigade's front.

the road. This was No Man's Land and the roof of a concrete shelter to the right of the path marks the site of Railway Redoubt **(3)**. Turning round to face south, it is now possible to view the area from the German perspective. Shelters were dug beneath the embankment and firing slits in either side provided an excellent field of fire. Mad Point is to the left; Madagascar Trench ran between the two machine gun posts. It is also worth having another look through the hawthorn bushes west of the track to see how the Germans viewed the Middlesex attack. Return to your vehicle.

Follow the path sign-posted for Quarry Cemetery **(4)**. From the entrance to the cemetery look north towards the houses of Cité Madagascar, which are partially obscured by a low ridge. Little Willie Trench ran along the top of the ridge **(C)**; Strongpoint, a concrete shelter in No Man's Land, was directly in front. A concealed ditch, filled with barbed wire and covered by turf, protected the German front line. The 6th Kings Own Scottish Borderers advanced parallel to the road, only to be confronted by the hidden ditch. They were decimated in a matter of minutes, raked with bullets from either flank.

Follow the track across the fields until it ends near the centre of 26 Brigade's front line, a distance of about 200 metres **(5)**. To the left is a huge sprawl of bushes and trees at the top of the slope; the site of Hohenzollern Redoubt. Lord Lochiel's 5th Cameron Highlanders occupied the ground to the left, facing Little Willie Trench and the north corner of the Redoubt. The Battalion's advance was delayed by ten minutes, after the men became engulfed in thick clouds of smoke. Many were struck down by the machine guns in Mad Point to the left as they approached Little Willie Trench. The 7th Seaforth Highlanders advanced quickly onto the Redoubt, taking the garrison by surprise.

26 Brigade's support trenches were to the right of the track. Throughout the morning they were filled with wounded and gassed men struggling to make their way to the rear. Meanwhile, 27 Brigade was trying to make its way forward to support the attack. During the afternoon the artillery occupied the slope, providing support for the troops near Haisnes village. The sight of thirty-six guns standing almost wheel to wheel in this exposed position would have been impressive.

Having taken time to visit Quarry Cemetery, return to your car.

Walking Tour 4 - Hohenzollern Redoubt and Little Willie Trench

Turn your vehicle around, heading back towards Auchy. Immediately after Mad Point, take the next right into Cité Madagascar **(1)**. The estate was built in post war years for the miners of Fosse 8. At the end of the street, where it turns sharp left next to a farm **(2)**, park your vehicle, making sure not to obstruct any properties. Take the track south, with the farmyard to your left, heading for Hohenzollern Redoubt.

The German main line crossed the track, from left to right, in 1915. Fosse Trench skirted the gardens of the estate houses to the right, and Mad Point can be seen about four hundred metres away. Little Willie Trench ran across the high ground on the horizon to the right of the track, joining Fosse Trench close to Mad Point. Dump Trench ran through the farmyard to the left and beyond.

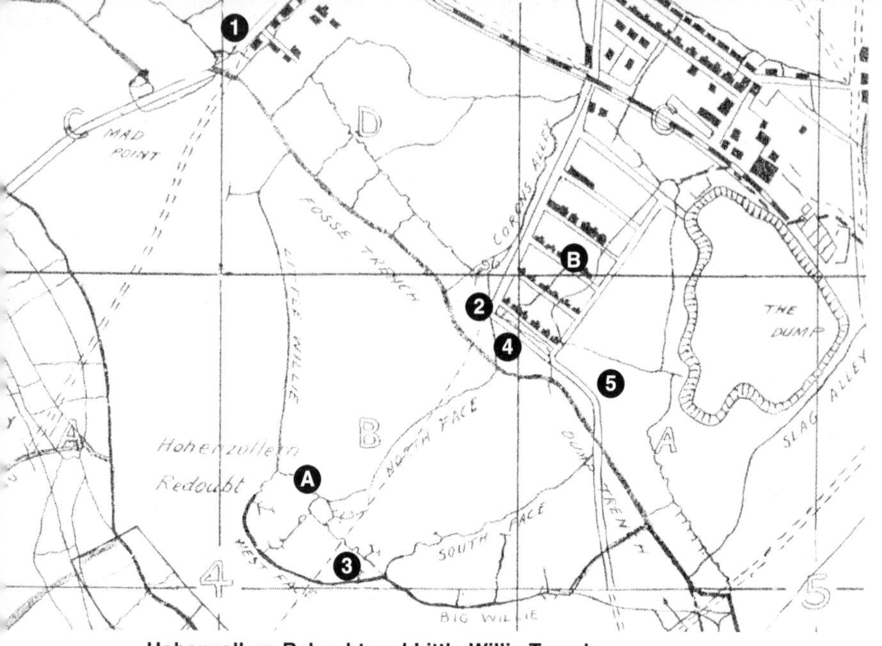

Hohenzollern Reboubt and Little Willie Trench.

The centre of the Redoubt is hidden under the clump of trees in front. East Face Trench (A) ran perpendicular to the track just before the trees. Two communications trenches connected the main trench with the redoubt. North Face ran along the left hand edge of the track; South Face crossed the field to the left. A great deal of fighting took place in this small area and it is worth getting your bearings before moving on.

On the opening day of the battle 26 Brigade advanced parallel with the track, as they headed towards Fosse 8, and many were struck down by machine gun fire from Mad Point. On 27 September 73 Brigade fell back in disarray from Fosse 8. They were rallied in East Face Trench by a mixed party of Scots led by Captain Fergus Bowes-Lyons. Although the Scots managed to fend off the German attack, Bowes-Lyons was killed. Major-General Thesiger also died in East Face Trench; killed by shellfire while observing the Fosse 8 position.

Continuing past the trees **(3)**; the ground levels out and a vast panorama of the battlefield opens up. It is obvious that the Redoubt provided the Germans with a grandstand view of the British rear area. On a clear day it is possible to view all of 7th Division and 9th Division's front line. In the distance the

Hohenzollern Redoubt possessed a commanding view over I Corps area.

ST MARY'S ADS CEMETERY

Area north of the Redoubt; for over for two weeks Little Willie was the scene of bitter fighting.

Vermelles - Hulluch road cuts across the fields. Alongside the road, half left near the horizon, a small clump of trees surrounds the Cross of Sacrifice of St Mary's ADS Cemetery. It stands in No Man's Land on the southern limit of I Corps attack. 7th Division's front line ran across the fields north of the road. On 25 September 9th Division held the ground immediately in front and to the right.

The Redoubt straddled the track with the fire trench, known as West Face, following the contour of the land in an arc. The trees to the left of the track hide some of the craters that the mining of March 1916 left behind. Nature has done a fine job of concealing the deep hollows, and I strongly recommend that you do not try to enter them. The edges of the craters are extremely steep and covered in undergrowth.

Between 28 September and 30 October 1915 the Redoubt was the scene of continuous fighting, typified by fierce bombing contests and incessant shelling. Eventually the Germans eventually regained the Redoubt, bombing their way along Little Willie Trench, through the maze of trenches until they were finally stopped at the end of Big Willie Trench.

Little Willie Trench ran back towards Mad Point, where there is now a heap of spoil. Fighting raged continuously here for three weeks. The fact that three Victoria Crosses were awarded for acts carried out defending the trench bear testimony to the ferocity of the bombing contests: Corporal James Pollock on 27 September, Second-Lieutenant Alfred Fleming-Sandes two days later and Captain Charles Vickers on 14 October.

Looking towards the gate of Quarry Cemetery to the right, the area immediately in front witnessed two night attacks on Little Willie Trench. On 1 October the 1st Welch managed to enter the trench, only to find themselves isolated. They were forced to evacuate Little Willie the following afternoon. An attempt by the 1st Suffolks on the night of the 2nd was a disaster, no one managed to reach the trench.

The final attempt to clear the Redoubt was carried out by 138 Brigade on 13 October. Before zero hour Corporal Dawson VC of the Special Brigade saved many from asphyxiation by dragging leaking cylinders into No Man's Land, immediately to your front. As you return to your vehicle consider the attack as both leading battalions advanced across the German front line. The 1/5th Lincolnshires and 1/4th Leicestershires advanced left and right of the track

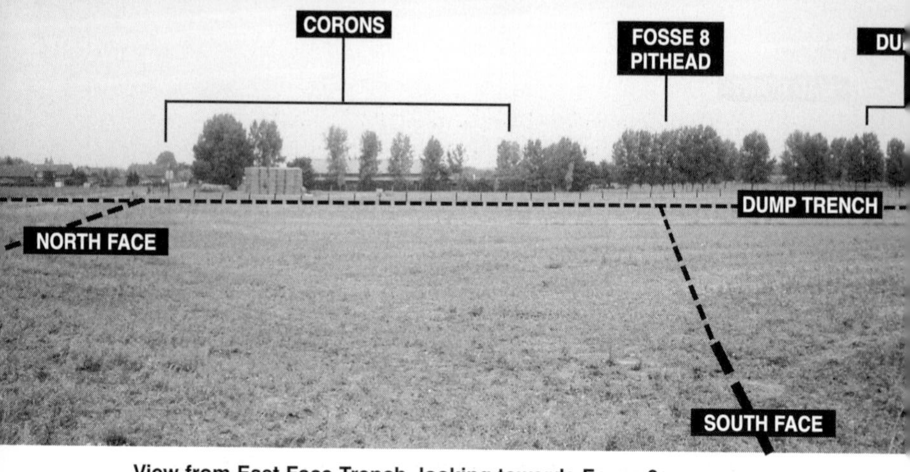

View from East Face Trench, looking towards Fosse 8.

respectively. They were decimated by crossfire from Mad Point to the left and South Face Trench on the right, and never reached Fosse Trench near the houses and farm. Captain Madge and a handful of men managed to take cover in North Face alongside the track, keeping the Germans at bay until darkness with a damaged machine gun.

At the corner of the estate **(4)**, turn right along a dirt track heading south east, with the farmyard to your right. Left of the track is where the colliery houses known as the Corons once stood **(B)**. On 25 September the 7th Seaforth Highlanders charged through the houses heading for the colliery. Two days later 73 Brigade ran for their lives in the opposite direction under heavy fire from machine guns on the Dump. Ironically the area is now a children's playground.

As you pass the farm, it possible to view the rear of Hohenzollern Redoubt, to the right. Dump Trench ran a few metres right of the track, while Big Willie Trench ran obliquely left to right across the fields. The Dump dominates the horizon to the left, but for now concentrate on the area to the right. A detailed inspection of the fighting for the slagheap is covered in the next walking tour.

Continuing east to where the track swings to the right **(5)**. It is now possible to distinguish between the Redoubt and a smaller group of trees and bushes, which stand on the line of Big Willie Trench, close to where it joined the Redoubt. On 8 October the Germans managed to drive the 3rd Grenadier Guards from the exposed position. Sergeant Oliver Brooks of the 3rd Coldstream Guards led a small party of bombers, retaking the lost trench. He received the Victoria Cross for his bravery and leadership.

As you return to your vehicle, it is possible to consider the attack made by 137 (Staffordshire) Brigade on 13 October 1915. The brigade start line was over three hundred metres to the south west and to reach the Dump the Staffordshires had five hundred metres of open ground to cross. They were met with intense machine gun fire from the slagheap as soon as they emerged from their trenches. Hardly anyone reached Big Willie Trench.

Walking Tour 5 - The Dump and Big Willie Trench

Head north through the estate, passing a sports centre on the right **(A)**. In 1915 the mine manger's house, where the Scots set up their headquarters on 25 September, stood here. Take the second right, opposite Relax Bar, onto Boulevard de la Fosse **(1)**. The houses were built on the site of the original cottages and mark the northern edge of the original Corons. A mixed party from 26 Brigade occupied the houses to the left of the road, facing Auchy-lès-Mines. At the end of the road are three large buildings surrounding Trois Cabarets junction **(2)**, and Tip-Top Bar maintains the tradition. Turn right down a narrow tarmac road, and park your vehicle in one of the two small laybys **(3)**. This track is a dead end, and not suitable for large vehicles as turning space is restricted.

The view to the left of the track is worth studying before visiting the Dump. The 12th Royal Scots crossed the open ground around 9.00am, moving right to left, heading for Haisnes which stands on the horizon. Nearly two hours later the leading two companies of 11th Royal Scots began to cross, but moved further to the north, mistaking Douvrin church for Haisnes church. On a clear day it is possible to see the two towers in the distance and appreciate how the error occurred. The second part of the Battalion followed the correct bearing and joined their sister battalion in Pekin Trench. It is easy to see why it was impossible to maintain the position in front of Haisnes. Once the Germans established themselves along the Auchy road to the left (the water tower and houses to the left now stand along it), they could sweep the open fields with machine gun fire. Fosse Alley ran along the track before cutting across the field, and the 8th Gordons held it watching as the Royal Scots moved towards Haisnes. Later that afternoon the Royal Scots fell back to occupy the trench.

The Dump, Big Willie Trench and Haisnes.

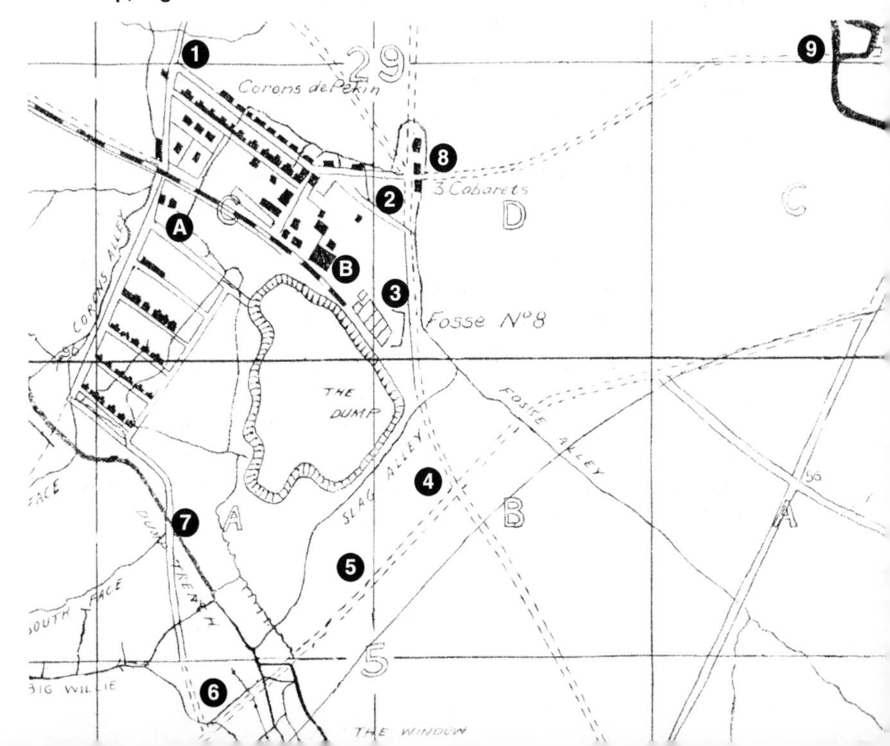

Looking along Big Willie Trench towards Hohenzollern Redoubt.

To the right of the lane, behind a concrete wall, is a large overgrown mound **(B)**. This is all that remains of the pithead tower of Fosse 8. Walking south along the tarmac track, it is impossible to ignore the industrial landscape to the right. Ever changing mounds of ash mark the northern edge of the Dump, and as a working tip it is impossible to enter. The shape and height of the Dump have obviously changed considerably over the years. Take care of the lorries that visit the site in working hours. Slag Alley ran along the eastern edge of the Dump. On the afternoon of 27 September the German infiltrated the 9th Royal Sussex near here, working left and right along Fosse Alley. Others moved down Slag Alley and onto the Dump. During the early hours of the following morning Second Lieutenant Alexander Turner bombed his way up Slag Alley, retaking 150 metres of the trench. He was mortally wounded, and posthumously awarded the Victoria Cross.

About 150 metres past the end of the Dump a dirt track joins from the right **(4)**, follow it keeping the slagheap to your right. It is only now that the size and importance of the Dump becomes apparent. Stop 50 metres short of the first electricity pylon **(5)** to study the eastern side of Hohenzollern Redoubt in relation to the Dump. The redoubt lies beneath the largest clump of trees to your half left. Big Willie started where you stand, running across the field to the left hand edge of the trees. Dump Trench ran in a straight line to the farmhouse, skirting the tip of the Dump. The 9th Royal Sussex fell back to this trench on 27 September having lost the Dump. Slag Alley joined Dump Trench in the field in front running to the right along the foot of the slagheap. The area to left of the track was covered by 7th Division and will be covered in the next tour.

One hundred metres past the pylon, a second dirt track joins from the right

East side of the Dump, Slag Alley ran along the base of the slagheap.

Area south of the Dump, scene of prolonged bombing contests.

(6). The junction is in a shallow depression in the ground, called 'The Kink' in 1916. Prior to the Somme battles it was known as the 'hottest place' on the Western Front. Overlooked by both the Redoubt and the slagheap it was an extremely vulnerable position. On 11 May 1916 the 13th Royal Scots lost half its number during an intense bombardment. The 18th Bavarian Regimental history describes the scene they found when the position was overrun;

> .... the British position was levelled, the dugouts crushed in, and the trenches strewn with corpses......

The Bavarians also captured several tunnel entrances and thirty-nine miners.

Follow the right hand track heading towards the farm buildings for about 200 metres **(7)**. On 28th September the 2nd Buffs charged from Dump Trench onto the slagheap in broad daylight; eleven machine guns cut them to pieces. The German counterattack succeeded in penetrating as far as Big Willie Trench, splitting the British line in two. The following day the Germans launched an attack as the 1st Yorks and Lancaster relieved the Buffs. In the chaos that followed the 3rd Middlesex evacuated Big Willie Trench, leaving the Yorks and Lancasters isolated. Private Samuel Harvey made thirty trips across this area carrying boxes of bombs to his comrades. He was eventually wounded and for his bravery received the Victoria Cross.

On 1 October the Germans struck again, splitting the 2nd Northumberland Fusiliers in two as they moved into Big Willie Trench. Desperate fighting continued unabated for the next forty-eight hours as both sides bombed furiously. The deadlock was broken on the morning of the 3rd, when German bombing teams systematically worked their way along Little Willie and through the Redoubt driving 84 Brigade before them. Many were forced to run to safety across to the left of the track, heading for the British trenches.

Walking Tour 6 - Trois Cabarets, Haisnes and Pekin Trench

Returning to your vehicle, continue on foot along the road to Trois Cabarets junction **(8)**. On the morning of 25 September 26 Brigade held the junction and the houses to the west along Boulevard de la Fosse. Corons Trench ran along the rear of the houses. The Germans held Auchy Cemetery, which can be seen along the road to the north. Later that night 73 Brigade arrived, and the 7th Northants took over the street, while two companies of the 12th Royal Fusiliers held the junction. On the morning of the 27th the Germans attacked, entering

Pekin Trench south of Haisnes. The Scots could neither advance nor retire.

the houses to the left, and the 9th Royal Sussex trenches near the Dump. To avoid being cut off the Fusiliers were forced to retire through the mining complex. Second Lieutenant John Easton wrote about the chaotic evacuation of Trois Cabarets in the third person, giving himself the name Broadchalk:

> Into this medley of shrapnel and bullets Morrell came running down the trench. "Get your men out, Mr Broadchalk, " he shouted. "You're cut off! Get those men out of that trench and make for the rear." A Company, left officer-less, looked up in bewilderment. Broadchalk jumped up on the parapet. "You get those men out". "I'll look after Number Eight platoon", shouted Morrell. "Come along men, hurry up."
>
> The appearance of Broadchalk was the signal for the German infantry to open fire: it was the first real target they had had. Behind him the walls splatted and hissed with the smack of bullets: he felt them whizz past his head and body. For fifty yards he ran, shouting to his men, hauling one up by the hand; then suddenly he cut through one of the houses and came into the gardens beyond, almost tumbling into Morell, who was running between the houses with what men from Number Eight he had been able to collect.
>
> There was no time to lose. The German front line was rushing over; the Germans on the left had driven in Number Eight, and were racing to close the gap: from the Dump there came the slow relentless pop of the Hotchkiss.

A track heads east across the fields towards Haisnes. Walking across the open ground it is easy to see how isolated the Royal Scots were on 25th September, once they had crossed the fields heading for Haisnes. Pekin Trench **(9)** ran to the west of the village, about 200 metres in front of the houses. By midday about two thousand men occupied a line north and south of the track facing the

Looking back from Pekin Trench to Fosse 8, the Scots were isolated with no chance of reinforcement.

village. With the Germans holding Haisnes in front and in force behind their left flank, (near the white water tower), it was impossible to make any further progress. The Royal Scots held their isolated position until nightfall, forced to retire when their ammunition ran out. The walk back to your vehicle will provide ample opportunity to view this part of the battlefield from the German perspective.

Walking Tour 7 - 7th Division's attack and Hulluch Quarries

Return to your vehicle and, turning round, head past Trois Cabarets and Auchy Cemetery into Auchy. Turn right at the main street. After a mile Haisnes is entered, again turn right onto the Lens road. Head south, passing Cité St Elie on the right, and turn right at a small roundabout for Vermelles. Elements of 7th Division reached this point on the morning of 25 September, the furthest point east reached by I Corps. Captain Findlay and about one hundred of the 2nd Gordon Highlanders reached what was then a crossroads. Soon after they arrived German reinforcements, marching in column, were seen approaching from the north. The Gordons' machine-guns scattered the Germans and many took cover in Cité St Elie.

After three-quarters of a mile there is a Commonwealth War Graves

7th Division's area and Hulluch Quarries.

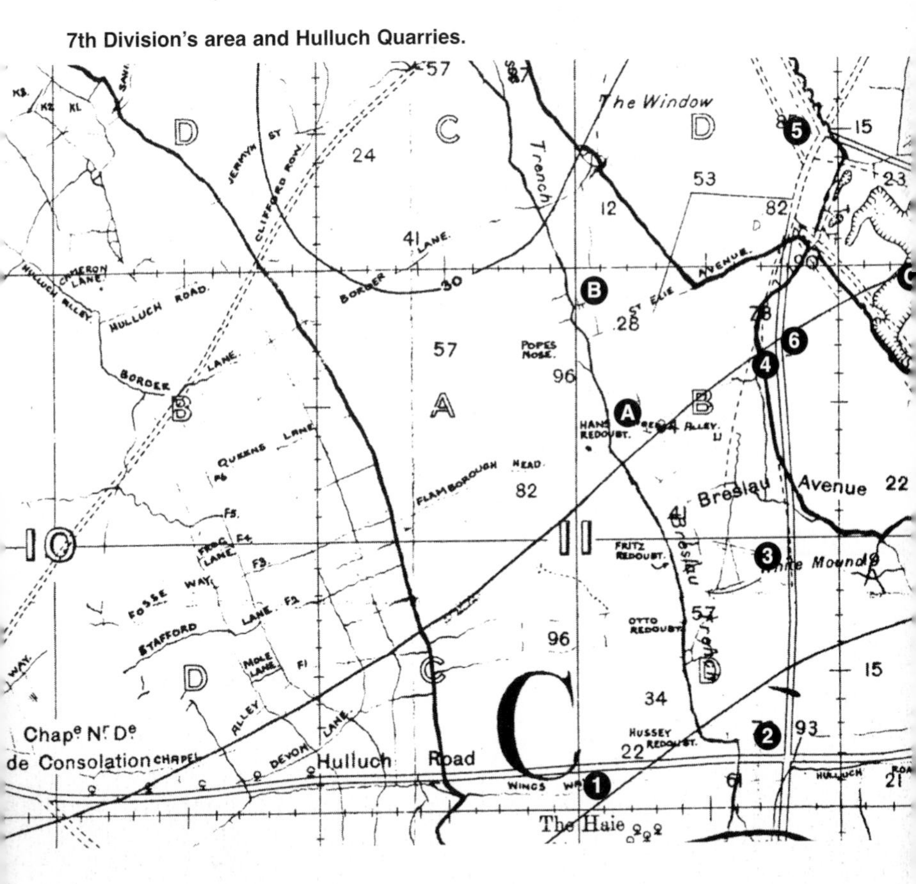

cemetery, St Marys ADS Cemetery, on the left **(1)**. Park your vehicle in the small layby in front of the Cross of Sacrifice.

After a visit to the cemetery take time to study the view north of the road. The cemetery is situated in what was No Man's Land, with the British to the left and the German trenches to the right. The road was the boundary between I Corps and IV Corps on 25 September 1915, and the ground immediately in front is where 20 Brigade attacked, with 22 Brigade beyond. In the distance the Dump can be seen, with Hohenzollern Redoubt to its left. The front line ran in a straight line from your left, towards the Redoubt, and prior to the battle 7th Division dug five lines of assembly trenches, halving the width of No Man's Land.

Walking east along the road, taking care of the traffic, make your way to the Commonwealth War Graves signpost **(2)**. Breslau trench crossed the road about fifty metres before the sign, with its support trench close to the sign. Crossing the road, take the track heading north behind the German line. The 2nd Gordon Highlanders came up the slope with their right flank on the road, piped forward by Piper Munro. Hussy Redoubt, which stood near the road, caused many casualties as the Gordons forced a way through the wire.

After about 400 metres a wall joins from the right **(3)**, following the track north. This was the centre of 20 Brigade's front. Fritz Redoubt was in the field 200 metres west of the track, with Silesia Sap beyond. The 8th Devonshires advanced too quickly, overtaking the gas cloud and suffered terribly near the wire, over seven hundred fell victim to the Redoubt's machine guns. Gun Trench, from where a gun battery shelled the advance, lay beyond the wall at the top of the slope.

Continuing north, the track forks at the end of the wall **(4)**; take the left hand path skirting the edge of the woodland and undergrowth. The front line ran through the trees after the battle and did not move for three years. Stop after two hundred yards, where there is an area of bushes left of the track, to look back towards St Marys ADS Cemetery. No Man's Land ran obliquely from the cemetery and in front of the bushes. A smaller clump of bushes stands isolated in the field close to the site of Slit Redoubt **(A)**. It held out during the initial attack

Looking south along the German line, 20 Brigade advanced from right to left.

German view of 7th Division's front.

and its machine guns fired into the backs of 20 Brigade's men as they advanced up the slope. Captains Sutcliffe and Ostle of the 2nd Borders returned from Gun Trench to take the strong point, capturing seventy prisoners.

Continue alongside the bushes, taking note of the position of Hohenzollern Redoubt and the Dump to the left. The 2nd South Staffordshires were pinned down in front of Pope's Nose Redoubt to your left **(B)**. Where the bushes end **(5)**, stop to look west across 22 Brigade's front. The roof of a small concrete shelter can be seen in the field in front. The Brigade came across the left front, stopping before the uncut wire protecting Quarry Trench. Only when the support battalion, the 1st Royal Welch Fusiliers, arrived was the advance resumed. Private Arthur Vickers, of the 2nd Royal Warwickshires, was awarded the Victoria Cross for cutting a way through the wire to the left of the small clump of trees in the middle distance. The brigade pushed forward through the strip of woodland to the left into the Quarries. Cité St Elie is hidden behind the huge slag heap. To the north is Haisnes village where the Scots of 9th Division became isolated in Pekin Trench

Turn around to make your way back to your vehicle. The return journey gives the opportunity to consider the subsequent fighting. After the loss of the Quarries on the night of 25 September, the British were back in the German support trenches near here. The following afternoon Carter's force, one and a half battalions 'borrowed' from 2nd Division, made a futile attempt to retake the Quarries. Major-General Thomson Capper, GOC 7th Division, led the force on horseback as far as he could, an obvious target in his general's braid. Dismounting near the British assembly trenches, he led until a sniper's bullet found his mark.

Major-General Capper.

For three weeks the situation hardly changed, both sides throwing all their reserves onto Hohenzollern Redoubt. On 13 October 1915 the 7th Suffolks and 7th Norfolks of 12th

Division made costly attacks against the Quarries. When smoke failed to protect the advance, they were swept by long range machine gun fire from the Dump. Captain Charles Sorley was killed leading the Suffolks bombers through the trenches known as the Hairpin. His body was never recovered, and his remains still lie beneath the trees to the left of the track. At the southern tip of the trees **(6)**, where a track joins from the left, look north. The wire fence surrounds a small quarry, the site of Hulluch Quarries in 1915 **(C)**. The land is private, and the undergrowth hides what little there is to see. On 13 October 1915 the 6th Buffs tried to advance across the ground to the east, attacking the Quarries from the south. Four hundred were cut down by crossfire.

Return to your vehicle and head west towards Vermelles. 46th Division's memorial stands in a small enclosure to the left of the road, just before the houses. From Vermelles, head south out of the village until you meet the N43, the main road linking Lens and Bethune. From here you can either head into Bethune to seek accommodation or head north to the channel ports. Alternatively head towards Lens, to pick up the motorway south to Arras and the Somme. Loos Memorial to the Missing, where many of the soldiers who died during the battle are remembered, stands alongside the Lens highway (about two and a half miles from the centre of Vermelles).

Chapter Thirteen

THE CEMETERIES

Bethune Town Cemetery

The Town Cemetery is located in the northern outskirts of Bethune, near to the Industrial Zone. There are over three thousand graves in the military plot at the northern end of the cemetery. Plots I and III were started in October 1914, shortly after British troops entered the town. Officers were buried in Plot I and Lieutenant Frank de Pass VC, of the 34th Poona Horse, is buried the first row. De Pass was killed on 25 November 1914 having thwarted a number of German attacks. During the bitter fighting he rescued a wounded sepoy under heavy fire. Meanwhile, other ranks were buried in Row A to I of Plot III.

Fabian Ware and Dr Stewart, members of the Red Cross, visited the cemetery in October 1914. According to Ware they 'found a small number of English graves all with plain but carefully made wooden crosses'. Following the visit, the Red Cross Mobile Unit began recording graves, and where possible, maintained them. It was the start of what eventually became the

Commonwealth War Graves Cemeteries in I Corps area.

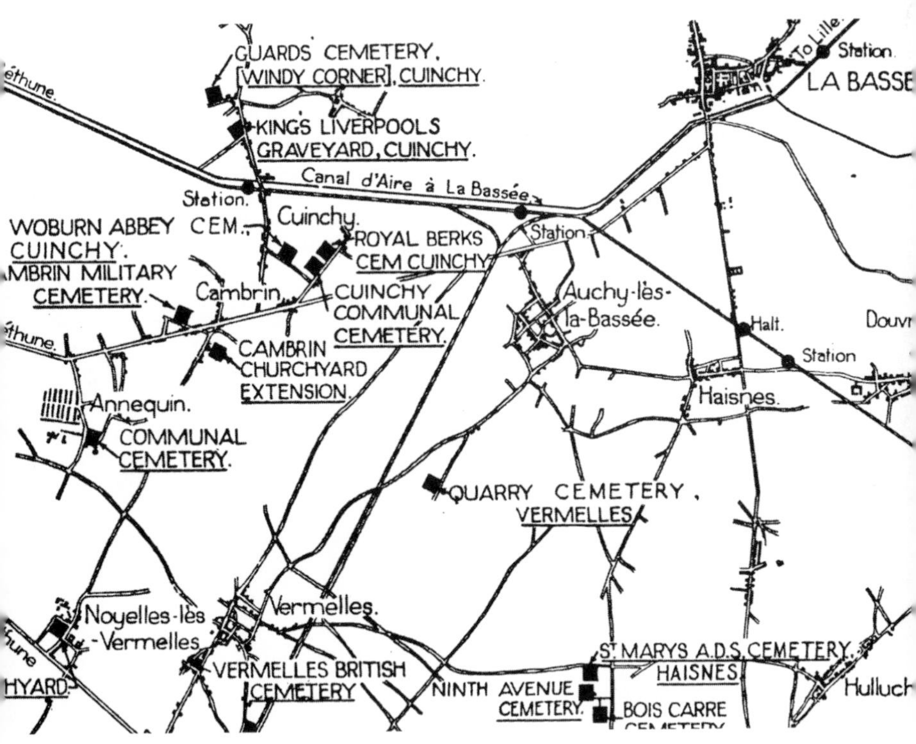

Bethune Town Cemetery.

Commonwealth War Graves Commission. Sir Fabian Ware headed the Commission from the beginning, leading it through its formative years. He retired after the Second World War.

The policy of creating separate plots for officers' graves continued in 1915. They were buried either in Plot II or at the back of Plot III. Lieutenant-Colonel Lord Crichton-Stuart, CO of the 6th Welch and son of the third Marquis of Bute, is buried in Plot III, Row M. He died of wounds received during the battle for Hohenzollern Redoubt.

Although the register states that CSM Hugh Hayes of the 2nd Welch died from accidental injuries in January 1915, he was murdered by two of his men. Privates Morgan and Price were executed a month later and are buried side by side in the first row of Plot IV. Robert Graves gives an account of the incident in his autobiography, Goodbye to All That. Hayes is buried in Plot III. Private

Walking wounded await evacuation, the tags give details of injuries and treatment. I Corps evacuated over 12,000 wounded in three days.

Bryant of the 10th Cheshire's is buried in the last row of Plot VI, he was shot for desertion in October 1917. Alongside Bryant's headstone is a mass grave of twenty-six soldiers of the 1/8th Manchesters. As 'D' Company marched through the streets of Bethune, looking forward to a festive break, the town was subjected to an air attack. Five bombs caused over sixty casualties among the Manchesters.

The Casualty Clearing Stations left Bethune soon afterwards and throughout 1918 the cemetery was hardly used. In September of that year Lieutenant-Colonel Lord Thynne DSO, a Member of Parliament and son of the Marquis of Bath, was buried in Row L of Plot II.

After the war several hundred French graves, dating from the first winter of the war, were removed from Plot III. Eighty-seven Germans prisoners who died of illness or injuries are buried in a separate group, alongside Plot II.

Cambrin Military Cemetery

Cambrin was only a short distance from the front-line and the houses and cellars sheltered a large number of men. One large house, known as the Mayor's House, was used by a succession of field ambulances to tend the wounded. Those who died were buried in the field behind, now known as Cambrin Military Cemetery. The first graves were made in February 1915, shortly after British troops took over this part of the front. One of the early graves is that of Captain Alan Fox of the Royal Flying Corps, one of the first of five Army officers who learnt to fly before the war. Fox was shot down on 9 May, observing the Battle of Aubers Ridge. 6 Brigade sent its casualties here on 25 September 1915 and many of the graves in rows C and D belong to the 1st King's and the 2nd South Staffords.

A large number of graves belong to miners of the 170th and the 251st Tunnelling Companies, they died in the underground war east of the village. Second Lieutenant Phillimore of the 251st Company, was an Exhibitioner at Christ Church, Oxford, before the war. He was killed in action beneath the French soil on 25 June 1916, age twenty. Two brothers killed together lie side by side in Row H. Private Thomas Matthews 33317, and Private Arthur Matthews 33318, of the 1st East Yorkshires died on 24 February 1917 when a mobile charge accidentally exploded, wrecking their billet house.

Cambrin Military Cemetery.

Cambrin Communal Cemetery Extension.

Cambrin Communal Cemetery Extension

The village church also housed a dressing station and the burial ground is dominated by a large military extension. French units buried over 150 men here in two small plots in October 1914. British units started to use the cemetery in May 1915, and continued to do so for nearly two years. One of the earliest casualties was Captain the Honourable Ernest Brabazon DSO, staff captain of 4 (Guards) Brigade. Brabazon died of wounds received during an attack at Givenchy in June 1915.

The church was home to the main dressing station of the 9th (Scottish) Division during the battle. It dealt with casualties from the 2nd Division as well as its own. Row C contains many graves of the 1st Cameron Highlanders and the 2nd Argylls, who were mortally wounded in the first attack. Most of the graves in Row H belong to soldiers of the 2nd Royal Welch Fusiliers and the 1st Middlesex. Many of the headstones mark two or sometimes three graves. The officers of the 7th Argylls were buried together in Row B. Further along the row is the headstone of Private Dupsanel of the 2nd Queen's. Dupsanel left Buenos Aires when war broke out and returned to England to enlist. Major William Hosley of the 6th KOSBs is buried in Row L. Command of the Battalion fell on Hosley's shoulders at the last moment, when his CO and adjutant were wounded. He too was wounded as he climbed onto the parapet, but refusing aid, continuing to direct operations until he collapsed.

By the end of the war there were over twelve hundred British graves in Cambrin churchyard.

Cuinchy Communal Cemtery

The village cemetery contains two plots. Plot I contains seven mass graves in a separate hedged enclosure next to the gate. Plot II, in the heart of the cemetery, is made up of three long rows intermingled with the civil graves, many of them scarred with shrapnel.

Two thirds of the men buried here were Guardsmen who died during the first week of February 1915 during fighting along the canal bank. On 1 February the Germans advanced along the railway embankment next to the canal, north of

Cuinchy Communal Cemetery.

Cuinchy. They managed to capture an advanced post of the 1st Irish Guards. Lance Corporal Michael O'Leary counter attacked alone, capturing two enemy barricades and killing a number of Germans. He was awarded the Victoria Cross soon afterwards, the first Irishman of the war to do so. The brave Guardsman was taken back to Ireland where he was treated as a national hero, and used as an example in the recruiting drive. His bravery led to many Irishmen enlisting for a country they were at odds with. Twenty two of O'Leary's comrades now lie buried in Cuinchy churchyard.

On 6 February Lord Cavan's 4 (Guards) Brigade launched a small but successful attack through the Brickstacks, straightening out the front line. Again a large number of Guardsmen were buried here after the attack. Many of the men would have been carried along Herts Avenue Trench, which connected Cambrin and Cuinchy with the front line. Twenty-five years later twelve more British soldiers were buried at Cuinchy, killed during the retreat to Dunkirk.

Woburn Abbey Cemetery

Woburn Abbey Cemetery is situated to the east of Cuinchy. Woburn Abbey was the name given to the adjacent house, used as a headquarters and aid post. The original plot, to the right of the gate, was started by the 2nd Division in June 1915. The 1st Royal North Lancashires buried seven of their number in Row G at the beginning of the month. They died when a mine destroyed a thirty metre section of the front line trench. The bodies of seven other men were never found. Nineteen men from the 16th (Church Lads Brigade) King's Royal Rifle Corps and the 19th (2nd Public Schools Battalion) Royal Fusiliers were buried in Row H at the beginning of 1916. The cemetery was abandoned shortly afterwards when the 2nd Division moved south, as later medical units

Woburn Abbey Cemetery.

Cuinchy New Cemetery, now known as Woburn Abbey Cemetery. IWM - Q56230

preferred to use of Cambrin. Only a handful of burials were made in the summer of 1917, and again in April 1918.

Four more plots were added after the war, bringing the total number of graves to 550. Twelve Canadian graves of the Manitoba Battalion were amongst them. Private Adamson of the Battalion was a captain in the Manitoba Dragoons when war broke out. He wanted to go overseas as soon as possible, and reverted to the ranks to make sure he was in the first contingent. Adamson's grave is situated in Row D, Plot II.

The communications trench which led back into Cuinchy village was known as Glasgow Street. A strongpoint known as Bradell Castle was situated in the field across the road. The trench leading north from here was known as Harley Street. The house at the far end of the trench, near the canal, was called Number One Harley Street, one of the most famous dressing stations in the area.

Quarry Cemetery

Quarry Cemetery is situated in the bottom of an old chalk pit, just behind the British front line. Dugouts tunnelled into the sides of the pit sheltered first aid posts and headquarters. Quarry Alley led east to the front line, while Quarry Boyau ran west towards the rear. Other trenches in the immediate vicinity were called Cromwell Road, High Street, Mud Alley, and Back Street. The first burials were made in June 1915, soon after this area came under British control. Nearly one hundred and fifty graves were made over the next twelve months.

Quarry Cemetery.

Although no graves date from the early stages of the Battle of Loos, several belong to the end of the battle. The graves in Row B bear the date 13 October 1915, the men dying in the final attack on Hohenzollern Redoubt.

Twenty-nine graves belong to cavalry regiments. During the winter of 1915-16 the cavalry divisions were dismounted and employed holding the line in this area. Several men of the 18th Hussars are buried together near the Cross of Sacrifice. The Germans blew a mine in front of the troopers' positions, destroying thirty metres of trench on 27 January 1916. When no attacks followed the regimental bombers occupied the crater while the position was connected to the front line and strengthened. It appears that the German tunnellers had got their measurements wrong, as the new crater gave the Hussars a distinct advantage over their adversaries.

No more burials were made after June 1916 and over the next two years shellfire caused a great deal of damage to the cemetery. After the war it was impossible to identify the exact location of many of the graves and the inscription; 'Buried near this spot' is carved at the top of many headstones. Despite its isolated location, Quarry Cemetery is well worth a visit. The secluded location is well cared for. The walls of the chalk pit have been planted with shrubs and flowers, converting this place of death into a beautiful garden of peace.

Annequin Communal Cemetery

There are only nine graves from the Great War in Annequin Communal Cemetery. An Indian soldier was buried on the north west side of the church on 31 October 1914, the first day of action for the Indians in this area. The remaining graves are situated on the south west side of the church. The 9th (Scottish) Division based their collecting post for walking wounded on the main road west during the Battle of Loos. Serious casualties were dealt with at Cambrin and Cuinchy. The village brewery was used by many British artillery units during the war. The upper storeys were used by the battery spotters. Meanwhile, the cellars housed the signallers and runners. Telegraph facilities connected the spotters to their respective units.

Vermelles British Cemetery

Throughout the war medical units used the cellars of Vermelles chateau to operate on the wounded. The village brewery performed a similar function. The 1st Gloucesters began to use the cemetery in the spring of 1915, when the battalion pioneers set out a small burial ground alongside a small French plot. 7th Division's casualty collecting post was stationed here on the opening day of the Loos offensive, and hundreds of wounded men were dealt with in the chateau. Those who died were buried in the chateau grounds. Most of the officers were buried in Plot I. A number of officers killed in the battle were buried in Plot VI, behind the Cross of Sacrifice. Three senior officers are buried here close together in Row D. The 2nd Wiltshires commanding officer, Lieutenant-Colonel Leatham DSO, was mortally wounded during the German attacks on Gun Trench in the early hours of 26 September. Captain Radford DSO, of the 1st Royal Berkshires died of wounds two days later. Lieutenant-Colonel John Monteith, of the 2nd Bedfords, died on 1 October. The 1st Coldstream Guards' commanding officer, Major (Temporary Lieutenant-Colonel) Arthur Egerton, is buried in Row G. His adjutant, Lieutenant the Honourable Maurice Browne, son of the Earl of Kenmore, is buried alongside. The Guards Division was engaged in a disastrous attack east of Loos on 27 September.

By the time the last Dressing Station left in April 1917, there were nearly two thousand graves at Vermelles Chateau. After the war a number of minor changes were made. Plots II, III and IV were completed by the addition of 167 graves cleared from small burial plots. Meanwhile, the French graves were relocated to the French National Cemetery at Notre-Dame-de-Lorette.

Eight artillery men are buried in Vermelles communal cemetery.

Dressing station in Vermelles. IWM - Q7253

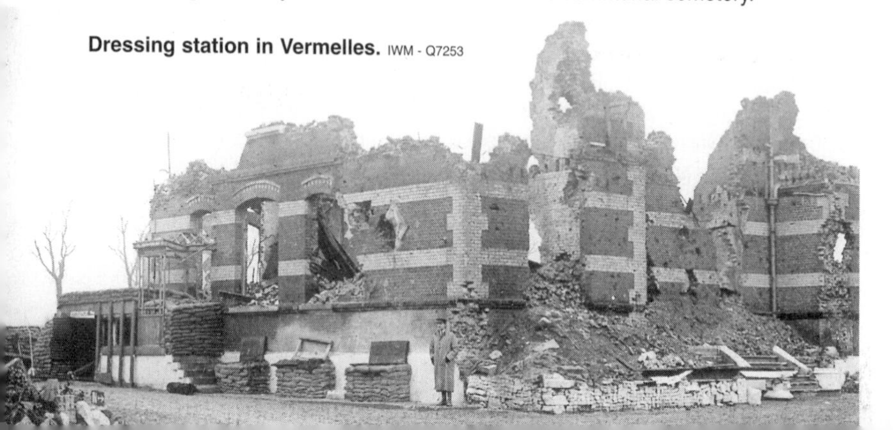

St Mary's ADS Cemetery

St Mary's ADS Cemetery stands alongside the road from Vermelles to Hulluch. An advanced dressing station (ADS) was established in the old front line trenches after 25th September. After the war the site was chosen for a concentration cemetery. It contains nearly 1,800 graves, of which only ten percent are fully identified. The majority died in September and October 1915. The Buff's, Kings Royal Rifle Corps, Devonshire's and Royal Sussex, who led the assault either side of the road, are particularly well represented. Twelve special memorials to the left of the War Stone remember seven officers of the 10th Gloucesters and five of the 1st Royal North Lancashires. The two battalions led the attack south of the road. They were all killed in action on 25 September 1915, and are known to be buried in the cemetery.

Lieutenant John Kipling, Rudyard's son, is buried in Plot VII. The death of this young officer influenced the appearance of the CWGCs memorials and cemeteries across the world.

Rudyard Kipling accompanied his son to the local recruitment depot on his seventeenth birthday, however, poor eyesight prevented John from being accepted. Undeterred, Rudyard contacted Lord Roberts, Colonel in Chief of the Irish Guards, to obtain a commission for his son. Within a year Second Lieutenant John Kipling accompanied the 2nd Irish Guards across the Channel, as they joined the new Guards Division. In less than five weeks, John was in action as the 2nd Guards Brigade tried unsuccessfully to attack Bois Hugo, to the east of Loos. Rudyard was devastated to discover that his son was reported missing, presumed dead. Despite extensive questioning, in part sponsored by his father, there was no conclusive news as to John's fate. Rudyard Kipling was haunted by the untimely death of his son until the end of his life. He wrote the following epitaph;

My son was killed while laughing at some jest, I would I knew
What is was, and it may serve me when jests are few.

The following year Kipling submitted a series of pieces for the Daily Telegraph in the wake of the Battle of Jutland. The first was a poem entitled 'My Boy Jack', a mother's lament for her son lost at sea; it was clearly based on his own personal grieving.

After the war Kipling became heavily involved in the work of the War Graves Commission and was very influential in the policy of marking the graves of unknown soldiers. In particular Kipling chose the inscription, Their name liveth for evermore for the Stone of Remembrance and the words inscribed on the

St Mary's ADS Cemetery.

graves of unknown soldiers. When parliament voiced its concerns over the cost of building extensive cemeteries and memorials in May 1920, Kipling addressed a large number of MPs who had served in the war to rally support:

> You see we shall never have any grave to go to. Our boy was missing at Loos. The ground is of course battered and mined past all hope of any trace being recovered. I wish some of the people who are making this trouble realised how more than fortunate they are to have a name on a headstone in a named place.

In the post-war years Kipling began writing the history of the Irish Guards, and in 1923 his two-volume work was published. Rudyard made several trips to France to oversee the early stages of the Commission's work. During the trips he and his wife, Carrie, spent many hours visiting cemeteries in the hope of finding their son's grave. Their searches were in vain and Rudyard died a broken man in January 1936.

In 1992 the Commonwealth War Graves Commission received information that a grave marked as a 'Lieutenant of the Guards' in St Mary's ADS Cemetery could be that of John Kipling. The Commission will only change a grave marker if there is conclusive evidence, and very few cases have been proved successfully. An investigation led to Plot VII, Row D, Grave 2 being given a new headstone inscribed with John's details.

The decision was made on the following grounds. The Irish Guards never returned to the Loos sector after October 1915. During their only stay in the area three officers of lieutenant rank died, Lieutenant Hines died of wounds in Vermelles Dressing station and is buried in a marked grave in the Military Cemetery. Meanwhile, Second Lieutenant Clifford was also posted missing following the attack on 27 September. During the post war clear up many bodies were partially identified by regimental badges or badges of rank on the tunics. (Metal identity tags did not appear until 1916.) The grave in St Mary's ADS Cemetery was originally marked 'A Lieutenant of the Irish Guards'; so by a process of deduction the grave must be John Kipling's.

The debate revolves around the date of Kipling's promotion to full lieutenant. By the time of his death he had not received formal notification of the commission. Supporters of the claim, reason that Kipling fastened the new 'stars' to his tunic in anticipation of the promotion. Others argue against the proposal. Either way, what is important is that young men like John Kipling gave their lives and they deserve to be remembered with honour.

After the war the French built a cemetery across the road and the remains of eight hundred poilus who died during the early months of the war were buried here. In 1922 the graves were moved a second time to Notre-Dame-de-Lorette National Cemetery.

Lieutenant John Kipling's grave.

FURTHER READING

Compared to many of the campaigns on the Western Front, the Battle of Loos has been overlooked. Although many of the unit histories written after the war contain short pieces, very few books relating to the battle have been published in recent years. The main source for extending your knowledge is the official account, recently reprinted and available from the Imperial War Museum. The relevant volume (Volume II 1915), is very detailed and it includes aspects of the offensive not covered in this book. For those of you wishing to expand your knowledge on the battle, the official account is the place to look.

Alan Clark's version, The Donkeys, is a critical history of the BEF in 1915. The section on Loos is concise and, as expected, the British High Command is given a rough ride. 1915, Death of Innocence by Lyn MacDonald follows the usual format with many personal accounts. The chapter on Loos gives a moving insight into what the fighting soldier went through.

In 1975 Philip Warner placed a request in the national press for personal accounts of the battle. His book, The Battle of Loos, followed. The work is an excellent piece of oral history, with many moving accounts of life in the trenches. It is, however, at times a confusing book, with many of the accounts relating to later campaigns.

Alexander Barrie's history of tunnelling on the Western Front, War Underground, contains a detailed chapter on the mining operations under Hohenzollern Redoubt. Finally, there are short pieces in two biographies mentioned in the text. Robert Graves Goodbye to All That and Frank Richards Old Soldiers Never Die served with the 2nd Royal Welch Fusiliers during 2nd Division's disastrous attack. Both give personal accounts of the build up and aftermath of the battle.

As yet there is no critical study dedicated to the battle. Hopefully, one day it will receive the attention that it deserves.

Military Operations, France and Belgium 1915, Volume 2
Brigadier-General J Edmonds, Macmillan 1927
Reprint available from the Imperial War Museum.

The Donkeys
Alan Clark, Hutchinson & Co Ltd - 1961
Mayflower-Dell paperback 1964

The Battle of Loos 1915
Philip Warner , William Kimber & Co Ltd - 1976
Wordsworth Editions Ltd - 2000

1915, Death of Innocence
Lyn MacDonald, Headline Book Publishing - 1993

War Underground
Alexander Barrie Frederick, Muller Ltd - 1962
W H Allen & Co Ltd paperback 1981

INDEX